The Ramblings of an Indian in South America

Nellie P Maan

Adrenaline Brush Ltd
PO Box 3565
Chester
UK

www.adrenalinebrush.co.uk

ISBN: 978-0-9559886-0-8

Wednesday 3rd August...

This morning the nine goldfish are discreetly making their appearance at the surface of the pond, taking gobs full of multicoloured fish flakes and diving for cover under the leaves of the budding water lilies. Their behaviour does not surprise me as I spot the heron high up in the cherry tree that is located at the bottom of the garden, next to the dilapidated double garage. As I sit on the low-level border wall on one side of the length of the pond, I admire the aged tree that still bears abundant fruit. I hope that one day I will get to pick some cherries, rather than the clean sticky stones left all over the bottom lawn and patio by the wood pigeons. My attention is distracted by the robin that has just flown home to its nest hidden deep in the Hawthorn tree opposite the cherry tree. The branches of the Hawthorn overhang both the neighbour's garage and mine. Several months ago I cut back the branches on my side to restore some balance and shape, as the neighbour's savage trimming exercise a year earlier had left the tree looking lopsided, shapeless and somewhat sad.

I turn my head back towards the pond and the green mesh netting that has successfully deterred the heron from taking the fish over the past 15 months. However, I now suspect that his interest is growing at the same rate as the fish that have tripled in size and are no longer invisible. I wonder if it is the same heron that obligingly emptied my pond two years earlier and tore the lining. I decide to see him off the premises using a handful of decorative Cumbrian stones that pave the area around the pond. I'm sure that I feel the presence of animal rights activists as each projectile is launched. Heron safely dispatched, I resume my seat on the wall, close my eyes and absorb the rays of the early morning sun. The noise from the distant A406 is gradually replaced by the flow of water that is being gently and rhythmically pumped into the pond. The flow of water is like the flow of thoughts through my head.

***

How are decisions really reached? Are final actions the result of conscious reflection, analysis and conclusion or simply the conscious manifestations of sub-conscious processes at work in the abyss of our brains? Is there such a thing as a brainwave or sudden inspiration or is it simply the conscious shutting up for a split second and letting the informed subconscious get a thought in edgeways? When and why did I decide to take off? When did the journey really begin? Maybe it began whilst tramping the mountains on South Island in New Zealand on a six-week holiday. I use the word holiday loosely as friends consider my vacations of choice as expensive experiences of physical pain and torture. During this trip, the brain was freed of meaningless meetings, endless e-mails and frying phones. In fact, it was emptied of everything to the extent that I was beginning to wonder if it had taken off somewhere and not told me. Then one day whilst lying idly on a sandy cove on Abel Tasmin and taking in the distant horizon the revelations started. They were not as dramatic as Paul's journey on the road to Damascus and I did not do anything crazy like find religion. I wish I could say that the revelations were like a comedy sketch by the sea with flying fish popping out of the water, slapping me in the face and diving back into the water. And with each slap came a new revelation. In reality, my revelations were like the waves rolling in from the distant horizon and gently coming to rest at my feet through the driftwood. I realised that I had been wrestling against the career ladder that had dominated my life for the past decade. My individual identity was being usurped by the social constructs of status, wealth and everything that represents modern living. The fight to be alive and living was being ground out of me and I was at great risk of becoming assimilated into the collective, the oneness of meaningless living. I was on the brink of becoming just another conformer of the epic work regime, waiting to retire at some vanishing point in the future. Even worse, I was being sucked into the life of a suit. As I reflected on these and other revelations I knew that I had travelled my journey as a suit and a new journey was on the distant horizon. From somewhere deep inside me, I heard the words of Confucius, 'A journey of a thousand miles begins with a single step,' – idly reading Confucius at the tender age of 16 had come back to haunt me or help me, I wasn't sure which.

So agreeing a redundancy package within 13 months of my return from New Zealand and three months earlier than the official end date of my nine years of time-limited contracts did not surprise me. I guess the work/life balance was restored in one swift move. Symbolically, I shed the physical suit for more casual attire, which at times raised a few eyebrows. Clearly the channel of communication between the conscious and subconscious remained alive and kicking and resisted all further attempts at assimilation. Along with the generous lump sum, I was sent a redundancy support and guidance package. What caught my eye were the bits about what to do next and the potential impact of redundancy. Let's start with what to do next. Well, you can get another job and whilst doing so apply to receive job seekers allowance. Right, so you are no longer classed as unemployed, just between jobs or job seeking. What an ingenious way of massaging the unemployment statistics. I wonder how much a suit was paid to come up with that idea. So what is the potential impact of redundancy? Depression was quoted as a possibility, resulting from the loss of position, status and income. Ironically, I was celebrating my loss of ascribed identity and threw a party. I wanted to celebrate as I had secured and used my get out of jail free card, got the bonus from the community chest and removed the shackles of wage slavery. Perhaps I was in a state of denial and a breakdown was around the corner. I contemplated what psychoanalysts would say and told my brain to remind me to ask some of my psycho friends over a soothing cup of hot chocolate. Reversing the assimilation process took time as I dutifully registered with a number of recruitment agencies and spent several days perfecting my CV. Apparently these are back in fashion. What next I asked myself, a handwriting exercise, in which case I would fail as the fine motor skills vanished with the advent of the voice recognition software. I even applied for a couple of jobs and attended an interview as well as explore my own business options. Morally, however, I could not justify receiving job seekers allowance and all the associated fringe benefits.

Now, as I meditate on my early morning actions, I wonder if I have fully recovered from the assimilation process. I woke up at 6am, opened my eyes, dragged my body out of bed, walked across the cluttered room, picked up a drawing pin, closed my eyes and stuck the pin into a faded old world map. I told myself that I would go wherever the pin took me. At first it was difficult to see my target as the pinhead obscured it or was it because I was still half-asleep. However, closer examination revealed that Ecuador was pierced. How is it possible to stick a pin in the little dot of a country that ordinarily evades the eye I asked myself? It could have been worse with Columbia and the ultimate adventure to the north and the Pacific Ocean to the west – a year out at sea. What if in reality the last nine years had been spent out at sea and I had only just begun to find land again! I observed that Ecuador is bounded on the south and east by Peru. So my left hand had decided that I was returning to one of the smallest countries in South America four years after my first trip. I remembered that Ecuador is named after the Spanish word for equator as it straddles the equator – not particularly original but at least logical. It is approximately the size of the UK with an estimated population of 13 million, the capital is Quito and the main language is Spanish. Most important of all it has mountains to die for or as my friends keep telling me to die on.

***

The splash of water disturbs the ramblings of my brain. I open my eyes and see the solitary frog that has just leapt into the water to cool off. I notice that the fish are now sun bathing near the surface, safe in the knowledge that the heron is no longer about. I'm finding that the fish are becoming increasingly difficult to identify. Consequently, the e-mails to my young niece Emma, who named most of them, are becoming stories of fiction. Bob is still golden with an orange spot on his head. 'Arry is still orange with a golden mark on his back. Splash, so called because she is golden with a tin of orange paint thrown over her, has also retained her distinction. Sophia is a paler beige and still fragile looking even though she scoffs a lot of flakes. Maxine, shortened to Max, is no longer the biggest fish in the pond and is turning a pale orange. Noire, who was jet black, is now bright orange and physically an identical twin to '7 of 9', so named because she was the 7th fish to leave the safety of the bucket and enter the pond. However, these two can be distinguished from their different behaviours. '7 of 9' has no fear and has just retrieved a fish flake from a newt. Noire is timid and typically waits for the leftovers. Lord Lucan and Lord Snowdon were missing and presumed dead until they reappeared from the depths of the water after about a year. Both had kept themselves well fed. One had turned into a larger version of Sophia and the other a pure golden colour. I had suggested calling them all Bob – it's what fish do – but it was difficult to convince the seven year old. Whilst keeping her big blue eyes on the fish she simply replied, 'Pas drôle,' and continued to choose the names. She photographed each one before releasing it into the pond.

Over a mug of freshly brewed coffee, I discuss my thoughts with the fish and pond life. The fish nod as they scoff more flakes – lazy buggers still haven't taken to the pellets despite being 18 months old, the toads are as laid back as ever and the newts seem to be full of excitement. With the downing of the last of the coffee, a mutual decision is reached. Today, on Wednesday 3rd of August, we have decided that I am taking a journey. So my post redundancy half-hearted attempts to search for work and explore business options resulted in a final decision to go to South America. As I continue to sit by the water, I am astounded by the amount of wild life that has attracted itself to the pond since I rebuilt it two years earlier. Pond skaters and water boatmen are present in abundance and dragonflies are circling my head. I am amazed at how all this life co-exists in perfect harmony. I am mesmerised by a spider that is weaving its web with scientific precision between the small metal arch at the bottom end of the pond that houses ivy and the hand-rail that runs the length of the pond directly opposite me. My sudden coughing bout shocks the poor spider who scuttles off to a place of safety. I leave it in peace and make my way towards the kitchen. For some reason I think of the Indian Prince, Siddhartha Gautama, who had left the safety of his Palace – perhaps he too was a free radical. Confucius has chipped in again with the words, 'If you want to get somewhere you must let yourself go.'

Friday 9th September…

It is the morning of Friday 9th September and I am admiring the garden from the top terrace having just returned from an energy sapping four mile timed run – it is only 8am and the heat is already insufferable. I like to appreciate the garden from different perspectives. Sometimes, I lie on my back on the bottom lawn and watch the movement of the clouds through the branches of the cherry tree. This is usually a good excuse to recover from a long run. Looking down the garden I can see that the summer bloom is gradually disappearing. I credit the previous owner for creating this 100-foot long and 20-foot wide oasis. It is planted full of seasonal flowers as well as flowering and non-flowering shrubs that provide a harmony of colour throughout the year. To my left, a grapevine and red wild roses cover the neighbour's extension wall. The fence down this side is covered with honeysuckle, clematis, three types of ivy and the ever-invasive Virginia creeper. A climbing hydrangea has claimed the extension wall to the right and is still flowering. The fence running down the right side is carpeted with ivy – yet another variety, passion flower, a climber with pretty flowers that has snuck over from the neighbour's garden, as well as more Virginia creeper.

Standing here, I realise that I will not be around for the autumn changes. I will miss life becoming peacefully dormant. I will miss the joy of seeing the cherry tree shower its leaves in complete abandonment. I am saddened as the winter frosts will come and go whilst I am away. Who will appreciate the spiders' webs when they are shown in all their glory by the early morning frosts? Even the early spring flowers and blossom may escape me. The glorious white blossom of the cherry tree contrasts beautifully with the pink blossom of the Hawthorne tree and provides a stunning carpet of confetti. I hope that my tenants will be cheered by it and take a moment to thank nature for its beauty. I am thankful that my redundancy has allowed me to fully appreciate the summer garden with its explosion of colour and fragrances that perfume the air – fragrances that often betray the secret presence of a flower.

Momentarily, I admire my own contributions to this oasis. Sir Matt Busby sits proudly alongside the other fuchsia bush and provides colour until the middle of October. The black beauty that I planted last year is an absolute sun queen and is thriving on it. The two new climbers with pretty flowers are blending well with the existing climbers. Since moving in, I have rescued both the top and bottom lawns from moss and weed – well actually there was more moss and weed than lawn. The top lawn is a perfect circle and the bottom a perfect rectangle. The Jones' would be so proud! The conifers that were taller than the house and choked by the Virginia creeper were usefully recycled. The asthma inducing lilies were given an early exit from the garden.

Before I depart, I will give nature an interfering hand and do the pruning. My annual battle with the ever invasive Virginia creeper that dominates the fences on both sides of the garden will take place after I have tackled the ivy. Unnoticed, some ivy has crept over the fences into the neighbouring gardens and I will need to retrieve the four foot long strands whilst the neighbours are out. The most challenging ivy is the cling-on which has to be prized off against its will.

I head towards my favourite seat by the pond. When conversing with the pond life, I prefer to sit on the border wall rather than on the bench just behind it. As I sit down I see that the water lilies are waking up gradually to the warmth of the early morning sun and stretching out their deep purplish petals over the green leaves that have spread across half the pond. I'm surprised that the lily has flowered – I put it in the pond at the end of May. I will need to remove it in the next few weeks as well as cut back the pond grass that has doubled over the last few months. I cast some flakes into the pond and soon there is a hive of activity. A pond skater has just escaped with a flake the size of its body but a newt is having none of it and is in there with the precision of a surgeon's knife. Before he can enjoy his ill gotten gains a bigger newt has helped himself. Ah, the harmony of pond life. As usual, I throw a few flakes under the flowing water as the loner Bob tends to hang out in that area. As usual, he turns up. All the creatures are patiently waiting for me to update them on the events of the last month. In the background the twittering robins and cooing pigeons are competing with the noise from the A406.

***

Straight after the last formal gathering, I went out for my daily dose of pollution. As I pounded the streets of London my brain posed further questions. When would I go? It had to be after the 25th Great North Run in

September, having spent a little time preparing for it. How long would I go for and what would I do there? Would I simply slum it around South America or do something worthwhile – not that slumming it is not worthwhile. Perhaps as a result of my subconscious and conscious rebellion against the suit regime, following my redundancy, I had also considered joining VSO – to live and work in India and apply the skills that I had acquired whilst turning into a suit. I had some fanciful idea of recovering and using my mother tongues. As I ran back up the street, past the tooting horn of a car that I tried to mow down, I decided that I would explore voluntary work opportunities in Ecuador. Consequently, I had spent several weeks searching the Internet for voluntary work in South America and discovered that opportunities existed in abundance, ranging from conservation and environmental projects through to social projects such as teaching and working with street children. There was even the possibility of working on the Galapagos Islands. The only drawback for the latter was the need to speak or learn to speak Spanish. I was somewhat perplexed by the need for Spanish when working with the giant tortoises but did not enquire any further. After much deliberation, I decided that I would do some voluntary work and learn some Spanish in Quito and take in some travel. Yesterday, I provisionally booked my schedule of activities with a company specialising in a gap year for grown ups.

The fish are listening attentively, the newts are swimming around excitedly, but the solitary frog is sitting quietly on the edge of the pond. I continue. Now for the difficult bit, telling people. Being the brave soul that I am, I thought it best to tell people nearer the time and now this leaves a month's notice. Over the weeks, friends and family have enquired after my future career plans. I have replied by saying that I am still exploring various options. However, during these moments of conversation the words of a Tracy Chapman song have kept playing through my head. 'She's got a ticket, I think she's gonna use it, I think she's gonna fly away.'

As the pond life continues to listen I explain that I am now attempting to contemplate all the questions and statements in advance of my big announcement. The first question will be three questions in one – why, why South America and why didn't you tell us any sooner? As I don't have any deep and meaningful explanation as to why other than that I don't want to be assimilated, a simple reply along the lines of a good opportunity to make the most of the natural break in my career will have to suffice. I know this sounds frightfully pedestrian but it will be more palatable than saying that I want to take a contemplative walk through life – besides I am likely to be told that I do too much of that anyway. So what can I say in response to why South America? For fear of being told I'm mad I can't really share my pin story, so I will fall back on my need to return to Ecuador and conquer Cotopaxi, having failed to reach the summit at the first attempt due to blisters. This time I know that I will probably have no chance due to the asthma, especially after seeing the look of horror on the face of my specialist when I informed her that I will be living at an altitude of 2,764 metres. I could add that I find the thought of being an Indian in South America faintly amusing. I will need to leave a few minutes for the nodding heads to come to rest before continuing to answer the question, why didn't you tell us any sooner? I will simply shrug my shoulders and say, 'It's just a generic trait that cannot be rectified.'

The next question will concern the length of my stay. To tell people that I have no idea is not a good idea, so I will play it safe by announcing my provisional return date and emphasise the short period of time that this really represents. Then there will be questions that people will have formulated in their minds but will not ask. Therefore there is no point in considering any answers. The statements too numerous to visit in detail will be emotionally challenging. These will be resolved with promises to keep in touch by e-mail and phone.

I will test the water this weekend and mention my plans to an old university friend, called Dom, who I know will give me his honest opinion. The frog suddenly croaks and I wait to see if he will offer any words of wisdom. He simply looks at me and hops off into the undergrowth. Was that a rather you than me look?

Friday 21st October…

I am heading for Heathrow airport having permitted myself 5 minutes of the Weakest Link – my last analysis of Anne's interaction with the human race for possibly six months. I would like to send her a list of my own one-liners. Instead of inventing even more, I use the time to mull over the events of the previous month or so. The journey up to this point has been rather like a journey on the Eurostar. Let me explain. The Eurostar leaves Waterloo and slowly makes its way to the channel tunnel as it negotiates various obstacles – going the right way, getting on the right track, waiting for the slower train to get off the track as well as the usual rail works and signal failures. However, once through the tunnel, you find yourself in Paris Gare du Nord before you've taken a breath. Having navigated my way through all my obstacles I was almost there. I broke the news to Dom a kilometre into the 10km run that we had agreed to do together – twenty years into our friendship that dates back to our teens and we still like to challenge each other. I sped off before catching his response as I figured he could take the next fifty minutes to digest the news. Much later, as I had finished the race 10 minutes before him, Dom told me that he thought that it was a splendid idea. He added that his brother Ben was teaching at a school in Quito and would be more than happy to put me up or put up with me, I can't recall which. Having not spoken to this poor chap for almost ten years I e-mailed him with my proposed plan. He was not only happy to host me but advised that I arrange my schedule of activities once in the country. So within days of finalising my plans I cancelled everything and my final plan consisted of nothing more than a flexible return ticket to Ecuador! Instilled with confidence after breaking the news to Dom, the next step was to inform everyone else of my plans – or rather lack of. Those dearest and closest to me I wanted to tell in person – others I was obliged to tell in person, which involved driving up and down the country. Some I phoned to break the news and some I simply e-mailed or told in passing. Some heard through the internet highway. Not surprisingly the news was better received by friends than family – perhaps I could write a best seller on how to successfully not fulfil family expectations. I had now walked many more steps of my journey.

By the 20th October my bags were packed and weighed a total of 50 kilos – merely 30 kilos over the strict weight allowance permitted by KLM. I could have gone Continental with the generous weight limit, but feared being sent back to England at Miami even though I was just passing through. I repacked everything and put 15 kilos in my flight bag and 5 kilos in a duty free carrier bag. A further kilo was on my feet in the shape of my Scarpa boots. The check-in luggage then weighed 29 kilos, only 9 kilos over the weight limit. I decided to push my luck at check-in and if challenged argue that the difference represented my lack of body weight, or that I was carrying my potential body weight outside of my body. This was not far from the truth as 10 kilos represented essential food supplies – one litre bottle of Ribena, Marmite, Branston Pickle, Patak Pastes as well as every dried spice needed for Asian cooking, Porridge oats, Yorkshire teabags, green tea and fresh coffee. The Patak Pastes were for my host for I consider it sacrilege to take such short cuts.

On the evening of the 20th I sat by the pond and said goodbye to the fish and the pond life. I told them that I had included a clause in the tenancy agreement that the fish must be fed daily and had stocked up on fish flakes. As I watched all the fish take the food, I noticed two or three small black shadows. They can't be newts I told myself. A closer inspection revealed that they were in fact baby fish. It was the next generation and the cycle of evolution had truly established itself within the pond. 'Life continues,' I muttered to myself as I walked away.

Sunday 23rd October...

It is 5.00am and I am wide-awake which makes complete sense given that the time in the UK is 11am. As the chances of going back to sleep are nil, I go in search of some paper to scribble down the experiences of the last two days. I find some checked paper and a black pen on the dining room table and return to the warmth of my bed. I departed from London Heathrow at 20.25 on KLM

Flight 1028. The young check-in clerk was so impressed with my travel itinerary that she did not note the excess weight and my luggage passed through without a hitch. The only thing left to worry about was whether it would actually follow me to Quito or vanish into some black hole at Amsterdam. KLM Flight 1028 was delayed and typically the connecting flight was on the far side of Amsterdam airport. Heavy laden, like a mad woman, I dashed around Amsterdam airport and entered the gate to KLM Flight 754 before the final call. When flight booking clerks say direct it need not necessarily mean direct, it could actually mean via other places. The plane landed twice, first in Bonaire and then in Guayaquil, before eventually landing in Quito at 8.00am on Saturday 22nd October. Fortunately, my luggage did not lag behind and arrived safely on the same flight.

The flight was full and because I booked so late I was allocated a seat in the middle section, with a German man to my left, two Swiss men to my right and two screaming babies just ahead. Usually, I secure a window seat against which I yoga my legs and sleep for several hours. Sleeping, watching a movie and reading an epic novel is my usual strategy to pass the time. On this occasion I was not likely to get any sleep, the movie list was bad beyond belief and I had left the latest Harry Potter book on the sofa. To pass a bit of time, well at least 10 minutes of a long haul flight, I sensibly changed into loose fitting clothing and slipped on my sexy surgical socks. Bored, I examined my expensive socks and wondered whether I was conned into believing that the chance of blood clots would be reduced. I thought, knowing my luck, one would squeeze through and do somersaults all the way to my heart. On such a busy flight there would be no room to place my body horizontally and I entertained the thought of being strung up vertically but boycotted further thoughts on the subject when I found myself eyeing the plane for places to put bodies.

I considered my options – listening to music, sketching, following the plane routine of eating gourmet food, drinking, buying duty free, dozing and eating again or talking to my fellow passengers. I did partake of the free wine, sensibly interspersed with water but declined the food when my stomach yelled out for mercy. I allowed the fair haired German, who lived in Quito, to pontificate about the country. He talked about the economic and political situation, the levels of crime and corruption and about his business and family. I learnt that the dollar was declared as the official currency in 2000 in response to the dramatic devaluation of the Sucre. Since its introduction, the cost of living had risen and the per capita GNP (gross national product) and GDP (gross domestic product) had consistently decreased year by year. Latest figures suggested that 75% of the Ecuadorian population remained unemployed or sub-employed and that the government was dedicating a sizeable portion of the nation's resources to keep up with interest payments on its external debt.

After the scheduled feeding break he continued even though I feigned sleep. I learnt that the main export commodities include petroleum, bananas, cocoa and cut flowers and the main export partners are the United States, Panama, Peru and Italy. Apparently the country's political instability that dates back to its independence in 1830 continues to the present day with presidents coming and going. He thought that organised crime such as drug trafficking, trafficking in human beings, trafficking in firearms, etc had more than likely increased as had crime against foreigners. Begging had become widespread. As I continued to listen, which I honestly did, I was tempted to ask if he had recently completed an MBA – the information that he provided sounded like a PEST analysis. However, I was well behaved and did not make any facetious remarks but I did order another wine. Hour by hour, I was becoming a very knowledgeable tourist even before the plane landed! In the end I was left confused as to who benefited from the dollar but my conclusion was that yet another poor country was being exploited.

The more this 35 year old imbibed the chattier he became and as he requested his sixth beer he commented that he had lost his shape and fitness and had gained weight. I smiled and nearly said that some women like their men chubby. He told me that he was married to an Ecuadorian woman, who worked on the radio as a presenter and had two young children who attended a German school. He was a general manager involved in exporting commodities to Europe. He offered me his business card and invited me to meet up for a coffee once I had settled in. I accepted the card without any promise to meet.

In the early hours he asked what I would be doing in Ecuador. When I replied, 'Contemplating,' he decided to get some sleep – why didn't he pose this question three hours earlier?

Intermittently, the Swiss to my right filled my lungs and the air with Eucalyptus oil and several times I reached out for my inhaler but alas he didn't get the message. From the peppered hair I deduced that he was in his forties. His face was disguised for most of the journey with tissues in various stages of decay. He explained that he had a bad cold and so will the entire plane I was minded to say but sympathy took over. His cold and limited English, combined with my non-existent German, reduced our conversation to the occasional smile and nod. Every strategy to fall asleep failed. Listening to the German chap failed, drinking wine failed and even counting the grey hairs on the head of the Swiss chap failed. Even the babies obligingly slept for a couple of hours before providing an early wake up call for the passengers and starting a screaming competition – each refusing to be out-done by the other. Unable to sleep, I told myself to prepare psychologically for the possible effects of altitude – a faster and pounding heart rate, breathlessness, headaches, light-headedness, nausea and a loss of appetite which can only be good news for anyone wishing to diet. For those who have not landed at high altitude, a common reaction is, 'Who the f--- taxed the oxygen?' but usually this is not voiced as you are too busy gasping for air. I decided that I was not going to get any of the symptoms; the mind was going to control the matter. Well it worked as I was asymptomatic and I even managed to avoid developing the Swiss cold, thanks perhaps to the Eucalyptus oil.

***

Ben was awaiting my exit from the Arrivals gate. At his request, I e-mailed him a mug shot in advance. The only recent one I had to hand was that of me fighting the clinging ivy off the cherry tree – the final pruning in preparation for the winter. I figured that given his towering height of 6ft 1" and the family resemblance, Ben would stand out from the crowd and he did. Although he had lost a lot of his hair, he had retained his good looks. I managed to stay awake for a couple of hours once arriving at the house, although I did not recall what he said other than he did not have a kettle and the cooker had exploded. I noted the damage inflicted by the gas flames on the wall above the kitchen window. The decorative dried chillies that hung across the top of the window had seen better days even before being consumed by the flames. I do remember my brain screaming, 'What no cup of Yorkshire Tea, but I've carried a box of 80 teabags across the world.' My brain was pleading, 'But the box of teabags is just in the flight bag waiting and wanting to be opened.' I did not voice my thoughts as I concluded that since Ben drunk neither tea nor coffee, he would not appreciate the catastrophic impact of this news. After a short walk around the block my body gave in and fell into a coma for four hours whilst Ben went out to his rugby practice. That evening I managed to socialise for a few hours with some of Ben's teacher friends before sleeping for a further seven hours.

Monday 24th October...

It is the morning of the third day of my new temporary life. I'm brewing over the weekend's activities whilst waiting for the kettle to boil – it takes an age because of the altitude. Saturday's priorities for Ben were to buy me a kettle, a cafétière and a large coffee mug. My cultural orientation began yesterday by watching a live football match at the local stadium. I decided to support El Nacional whilst out here because this was one of the two teams playing on the day and the players wore a red kit. My rational for choosing this team was as irrational as choosing to support Manchester United as a child. For some inexplicable reason I had acquired the label 'little devil' and accidentally discovered that a football team was called the Red Devils. With a smile on my face, I adopted both the team and the label 'a little red devil'. Much to my parents' horror, I also developed a passion for playing the game. In a state of panic my mother asked, 'What will the neighbours say when they see an Asian girl playing football?'

When I replied, 'They've already invited me to join the boys' team,' she was actually lost for words and never raised the matter again. At the time I wondered why she was concerned about the neighbours. All this was about 20 years before the film, 'Bend it like Beckham,' was released. Watching the film, I wondered if my mother perhaps meant the Asian neighbours. But there were none!

The other team was dressed in a horrid yellow and called Deportivo Quito. As we watched the game, Ben kindly provided a running commentary on football in Ecuador and my chosen team. The Ecuadorian league is the equivalent of the English Premiership but a somewhat different standard. My new temporary team is officially known as Club Deportivo El Nacional and is from Quito. It belongs to the Ecuadorian military and only players with an Ecuadorian nationality are allowed to play for the team. The kit colours of red, dark and light blue represent the three branches of the military. As the team was playing on its home turf I deduced that the home kit is red. I was amazed to hear that El Nacional is one of the leading teams in Ecuador and in the past had reached the quarterfinals in the South American Championships – the 'Copa Libertadores'. The team played dreadfully and deserved to lose. The final score was 2:1 to Deportivo Quito. Alan Hanson would have been shaking his head and saying, 'Given away cheaply again and again,' 'Lacking conviction,' and 'A very disappointing game.'

The stadium was less than half full, probably due to cost. With an average monthly salary of approximately $280 even the cheapest tickets at $5 are likely to be prohibitively expensive for many locals. Despite this, there was a lively atmosphere. From time to time during the match my attention was drawn to all the other activities within the stadium. Vendors walked around selling ice cream, hot dogs, cooked meats, bubbles, beers and soft drinks as well as a range of memorabilia. Watching football here is a family affair and I watched mothers and fathers share their passion for the game with their children. During the interval the shoeshine boys were out in force. With a smile they moved on quickly from me as I was wearing trainers.

After the match, Ben and I went for lunch and took a trip around the area. I recognised Mariscal Sucre, the sector locally known as Gringo land and the area where most tourists spend their time. Not surprisingly, it has a high concentration of travel agencies, hostels, restaurants, bars, and Spanish schools. The place had hardly changed and was full of overseas travellers.

***

I take my coffee and return to the warmth of my new and temporary single bed. I sip slowly from the large mug and take in more of my surroundings – the jet lag must be subsiding. The room, which is approximately 11 foot by 10 foot, has polished wooden floorboards running down its length. My bags are still lying half-opened in the corner opposite the lopsided doorway. The width of the wall adjacent to the bedroom door has a fitted stained wooden wardrobe and slightly slanting open shelving units. The wall opposite the wardrobe, like the ceiling, is painted a dazzling white. The external wall down the length of the room is taken up by a barred window and my creaky bed. The wall opposite is painted batman blue and I wonder if it was once a child's room. Coincidentally, my blue bedding blends in beautifully with the wall. On the edge of the bed I notice the A3 photocopy of a map that Ben has left for me so that I can orientate myself.

As soon as I write the last sentence I find myself drifting off into the early morning cloudless sky. My mind is exploring life and life maps. Isn't life like a map or a series of maps? Some people get simple ones that are clearly demarcated, others receive OS maps with or without a compass, some just get an Ariel photograph of their world and some have no maps at all – are these people the luckiest of all. Do people take the time to examine their life maps? Do they ever question their life maps; do they ever change their life maps for different ones? Do they try and make sense of their journeys and reach some meaningful conclusion? Ultimately, can't it be said that life is just a collection of journeys travelled? Over the years I have used many maps and travelled many journeys. Sometimes I have swapped maps with others or just accompanied them on their journeys. At other times, I have invited people to journey with me. I am now on a new journey, a journey that will be shared with new people and new cultures.

I suddenly find myself returning to the real world as I sip cold coffee. I was clearly away for a while.

***

It is mid afternoon and I have returned from my twofold mission of finding a Spanish school and familiarising myself with the area – the streets, the buildings and the heartbeat of life. Armed with the A3 map I had let myself out of the house and the bluish-grey front metal gate. I had written the address – Pontevedra – on the map so that I could find my way back. I remembered from the evening before to turn right out of the front gate, right into Lerida, right into Toleda, left onto Madrid and then straight down to the main road called the Avenida de 12 de Octubre. Off this main road are all the roads that lead to Gringo land. I had studied the map carefully before leaving the house as I certainly did not want to be the stereotypical newly arrived tourist who stands on street corners trying to work out which way to go. All the way to the 12 de Octubre I made a mental note of the landmarks. First was the restaurant at the end of Pontevedra with its multicoloured six-inch square glass windows. The football pitch opposite the end of Lerida was drawn to my attention as a group of lads kicked their ball into the dual carriageway on Toledo – sadly it met an untimely death under the wheels of a bus that was chucking out clouds of grey pollution. They looked at me pleadingly, but I took one look at the speeding traffic and shrugged my shoulders. There was a little skinny man selling the national paper, El Comercio, on this central reservation. As I walked past, I imagined tomorrow's headline if I had tried to rescue the ball – 'Woman and football scraped off road.' On Madrid there was a long ugly grey waterfall – probably another regrettable millennium relic, a shoe shiner, a man selling drinks and a disabled, barefooted beggar. Once on the 12 de Octubre, I turned left and continued walking. I noted the university and many well dressed students, more street vendors, rifle swinging security guards, stray dogs and stray children as well as a range of restaurants and shops. On the corner of Jorge Washington and the 12 de Octubre I spotted a woman with a baby that was wrapped in a blanket and tied to her back. She was selling a range of small sweets from the top of a foot square cardboard box. I greeted her as I turned into Jorge Washington and ticked her off as another land feature.

I soon found my destination, the South American Explorers Club – commonly know as SAE. I paid my fee and signed up as it afforded me free access to the Internet, information, books and guides, free refreshments and a place to hang out and meet fellow travellers. There was a weekly e-mail newsletter and membership entitled me to a 5%-10% discount at many Spanish schools. Afterwards I trudged up and down a few streets trying to find the recommended Spanish school, which I eventually did with the help of a rather attractive American guy who went out of his way to speak to people in Spanish and point me in the right direction. Later on we bumped into each other again and spoke briefly. I never saw him again after that encounter. I received a 5% discount at the Spanish school and I signed up for 40 hours over a period of a fortnight, almost the equivalent of a years worth of evening classes back in the UK. I would be doing four hours a day, five days a week and agreed to start on Wednesday morning. Given that my concentration span is less than 20 minutes at a time, concentrating for four hours on a one-to-one with only a 30-minute break would prove challenging. There would be no chance of slipping in and out of the class mentally without being noticed. In passing, I was introduced to Mercedes, my Spanish teacher. She is a woman in her thirties and no more than 5 foot in height.

Continuing with my familiarisation exercise I found that there were many places that I recognised in the so-called Gringo land. I remembered the Magic Bean café and went in search of it to have a drink for old time sake. This was a café that I frequented several times with a friend during my previous visit to the country. In my next e-mail I would let her know that little had changed over time – I couldn't decide whether this was a good thing or not. She had decided to take a year out to do voluntary work in India. The Magic Bean reminded me of the timeless Coffee Time café in Ambleside in the Lake District. This was my café of choice since my student days as it served coffee in cafétières dressed in waistcoats and provided egg timers so that you could plunge the plunger once the coffee had brewed for the correct amount of time.

It can be described as a very old style kind of place that was furnished with dark wooden furniture and shelving that displayed world coffees. Classical music frequently played in the background. It was the prefect place to come for coffee and cake after a weekend in the hills. The owner seemed an ageless and timeless kind of person who always sat at the till and never smiled and over 15 years became as permanent as the hills. Two years ago the place changed hands and became a modern characterless café with a pass code for the toilet and perhaps more suited to London than the Lakes. After my first visit I vowed never to frequent it again.

***

It's nearly 5pm and starting at the front gate I decide to walk through the whole house – except Ben's room of course. Ben's single storey house, which he is renting for a period of six months, is behind an eight-foot high double fronted gate and at the bottom of a thirty-foot part grass and part paved drive. Walking down the drive I notice the local fruit bushes – some belong to Ben and others overhang from the Neighbour's house. I pick fruit from each of the bushes to use in a compositional sketch – I intend to improve my sketching skills. The drive opens up into a wide courtyard that runs down the front, left side and back of the house. The front courtyard has a number of flowerbeds containing flowers and bushes at different stages of bloom. One of these flowerbeds would certainly make a great six foot by three foot pond. As I walk around the side of the house the strong scent of the lilies gives them away. At the back I find the kitchen door – as it is locked I retrace my steps to the front entrance.

The entrance leads straight into the living/dining room and divides it equally – the living area is to the right and the dining area to the left. On either side of the entrance is a large window. The windows and the door have black metal prison like bars on the outside. In fact every door and window is similarly barred on the outside. The room is about 25 feet in length with wooden flooring similar to my bedroom running down the length of the room itself. An archway on the left side of the room leads to the bathroom, the bedrooms and the chill out room that contains a dartboard and hooks for a hammock, but no hammock. Coming back into the living room, on the wall opposite the archway is an oil painting of a group of people walking into a rich golden sunset at the end of a fiesta. It is very well executed and invites the observer to join the group into the horizon. I would happily hang this painting in my house. The dining area consists of a wicker style, glass top, dining table and four dining chairs. A dark wooden desk rests against the wall opposite the window and houses the computer. On this wall is a triptych painted in brown and orange oil paint that depicts Mount Cotopaxi and the surrounding area – I'm not too enamoured by this painting. The living area consists of a two-seat wicker sofa – which I can lie on quite comfortably – two wicker armchairs and in the corner there is a television, DVD and CD player. Diagonally opposite the front door is the entrance to the large kitchen/dining room – a room that will be a place of culinary destruction once the cooker is fixed.

Tuesday 25th October...

It is early in the morning and I am sitting at the desk drinking coffee and checking out the Internet connection that has just been installed. With cable TV fitted on Saturday and the Internet today, it is like being back in the UK. The two workmen that have just left didn't seem convinced that I spoke no Spanish and seemed even less convinced when I said I was from England. My first e-mail is to Ben to let him know that we are now on line. My in-tray is full of e-mails from people back at home – I've only been gone four days. However, the one that I read first is the electronic newsletter from the SAE club as it is my first local e-mail. The newsletter contains all sorts of useful and useless information. I smile to myself as I read about the forthcoming monthly pub quiz at the British Pub. A British Pub in Quito, why doesn't this surprise me! I will suggest to Ben that we go along for a laugh. The bit that particularly catches my attention is the need for volunteers to visit overseas prisoners. The visits take place every Wednesday afternoon to the El Incas women's prison. Knowing absolutely nothing about what would be involved other than I needed to bring my passport, I phone up and offer my services – talk about starting at the shallow end of voluntary work. As soon as I put the telephone down my anxiety levels are off the scale. I have never visited a prison overseas but have heard all kinds of horror stories. My brain cells are bouncing all around my skull and throwing all sorts of questions at me. Once inside will you get out again? Will your anxiety be written across your face? What will you say, what will you offer? What sort of people will you meet? What conditions will you encounter? Will you feel safe? To bring the brain back under control I treat it to a pint size mug of Yorkshire tealiciousness – I have rationed myself to using one tea bag a day, as it is not possible to buy Yorkshire Tea bags out here. Aye, nowt beats a cup of Yorkshire tea, made from tea leaves grown on those Yorkshire Moors and hand picked by those fair maidens. Aye! So tomorrow I will be undertaking four hours of Spanish and a prison visit. After dealing with half the e-mails, I can no longer resist the blue skies and sunshine and go out to explore my neighbourhood.

***

As I step out of the front gate, I look down the hill and notice that the house two doors down on the right has an old rusty sign that reads, 'Villa Darshan Singh.' I am tempted to go and knock on the door and say, 'Sat Sri Akal,' which literally means that God is True and Timeless and is the formal Sikh greeting. Personally I prefer to say, 'Kiddha,' – an informal non-religious greeting that can roughly be translated into Yorkshire as 'Ay-up.' I resist the temptation and instead walk up the hill to Madrid. Here I turn right and explore the range of shops on both sides of the street – Internet Cafés, iron mongers, car mechanics, gas suppliers, restaurants full of locals, a mini market and the usual corner shop that is not owned by Asians.

As I walk around the residential streets I realise that everyone lives behind high walls and metal or barred gates and most residents seem to have vicious looking and sounding dogs. Just like Ben's house, most windows have bars on the outside. Several times my body leaps out of my skin as dogs jump up against the gates unexpectedly. At this rate I could develop a real dislike for these creatures. As I utter these words I can feel my poor pet dog Thomas turning in his grave in disapproval – I find myself apologising to him. Most streets have small telephone sized wooden huts that house guards with guns. In fact guns and riffles are very common. Security and safety is clearly high on people's list of priorities but I can't help but feel that people are prisoners in their own homes. Suddenly my tired legs are reminding me that Quito is a very hilly city so I head back – I look out for Cotopaxi, which Ben assures me can be seen from the top of the street, but alas, all I see are distant clouds. Perhaps he's joking.

Wednesday 26th October…

It is 5.30pm and I am sitting on the sofa having just said goodbye to Ben's cleaner Gladys. Gladys cleans the house and does the laundry and ironing once a week. Probably in her fifties, she is a plump woman whose plumpness suits her. I liked her warm and welcoming smile. I was unable to say much to her other than hello and I am Ben's friend from England. However, this didn't stop the poor woman from chatting away. The only bits I understood were, 'Si, si – yes, yes,' and 'Yo sé – I know.'

Sipping tea I find myself staring at the two black prison visitor stamps on my forearm. I am unable to make out the symbols or the ineligible writing. After a sleepless night worrying about the unknown I did go through with my commitment. With a head full of Spanish, I walked down the street past the national police station to the SAE to meet the group that would be going on the visit. As I stood in the foyer waiting for the group to get ready I considered what motivated each person to do the visit. Was it curiosity, the experience, the need to support fellow countrywomen or some other reason? I sensed that everyone was anxious. Eventually, armed with bags of essential goods – toiletries, clothes, etc – we all headed off to catch the Ecovia to Rio Coca on the Avenida de 6 de Deciembre.

This was my first experience of public transport and my second new experience of the day. I was told that the Ecovia is a bus service that runs in a dedicated bus lane along the 6 de Deciembre from Rio Coca to La Marina.

Along the route there are a number of sheltered stops at regular intervals. You put 25 centavos in the coin operated turnstiles to get on the bus. The bus was packed with less than standing room by the time it reached Rio Coca. The funniest moment was when one bloke got on and shouted, 'Perdón, permisso,' and tried to pass through a mass of bodies compressed together to some imaginary space that only he could see. 'No,' was the choral response from the locals that tonally could be translated as, 'No you can't bloody pass.' All this I observed from the comfort of a seat behind a metal handrail, right next to the exit.

From the bus terminal we took a short yellow taxi ride to the gates of the prison itself. There was a very long queue of local people waiting to go in. The group leader gave us names of overseas prisoners that we needed to give to the prison officials. We had to remember both a name and country of origin. She also informed us that we would be stamped twice on the left arm. It was imperative that both stamps were on the same arm – otherwise we would not be allowed to leave. Five minutes later and just as we were about to be admitted, we were told that the right arm would be stamped. I wanted to say, 'Are you sure?' but instead I quickly rolled down my left sleeve and rolled up my right one as I didn't want to get this bit wrong. I stood in the middle of the group and watched the process carefully. At the window of the first wooden hut passports were handed in and arms stamped once. The little uniformed man examined my passport, looked at my photograph, stared up at me and then at my photograph again. I wanted to say, 'I really am British and honest that really is me, it's just a 6 year old photograph,' but found that silence prevailed. I pleaded with God that the passport would not go astray. I watched as the male visitors proceeded to a hut on the right and women to one on the left. Here the bags of goods were checked and everyone was searched. The female guard found my inhaler during the body search and asked what it was. Unfortunately, my first four hours of Spanish did not quite equip me with the relevant words and phrases and my fellow visitors simply shrugged their shoulders to indicate that they could not help. Comically I mimicked taking my inhaler, grabbing my chest and pretending to breathe awkwardly and from somewhere uttered, 'Es necesario para mi,' shocking both myself and my fellow visitors to whom I had declared that I did not speak any Spanish. The guard smiled as she returned my inhaler. I was glad to provide a few moments of light relief and a story that would no doubt be recounted to friends and relatives. Later, I was told that the previous week the group explained the function of tampons, which brought a smile to my face.

After the search our arms were stamped again and we were allowed through a second prison gate, which opened up into a long and wide mud courtyard. Immediately I was overwhelmed by the sheer number of people milling about. It was like being on the tube in London at peak times with no room to move. I noticed that there were no obvious meeting rooms and everyone just mingled. Couples and families were congregating in any bit of space that they could find and I could not distinguish the female visitors from the inmates. Children were moving about without fear of being crushed or lost in the crowds. Within a few moments the white visitors attracted the attention of the local prisoners and were approached for money. I watched as some gave kindly and others refused. The noise level was almost maddening and just as I was beginning to question the merits of the visit, the group was dragged through the crowds to the only room at the end of the courtyard. Thankfully it was empty and my sanity welcomed the silence.

The bags of goods were taken and spread out on a wooden table and the prisoners helped themselves as they entered the room to meet us. No one behaved in a selfish or greedy manner and the women took only what they needed. We sat down on benches around some long tables and introduced ourselves to the handful of prisoners that wanted contact with overseas visitors. All the women were from Europe and America and serving long sentences for drug trafficking. I spent my time listening to a woman whom I shall refer to as Faith. Faith was a good-looking woman of mixed heritage and no more than 30 years of age. Although good-natured and caring, she was a tough cookie with influence amongst the other prisoners. When local prisoners entered the room she gently but firmly persuaded them to leave. To the neediest she gave provisions.

Faith wanted to share her story and asked that we share it widely to stop others from doing what she did. Following the events of 9/11 in New York,

Faith lost her job and discovered that her husband had not paid the rent for four months which amounted to over $4,000 of arrears. With four young children, bailiffs at the door, and mounting debt, desperation took over and Faith turned to a friend for help. This friend put her in touch with someone who offered her money in exchange for a drugs run to Ecuador. Her family knew nothing of her intentions and she simply told them that she was going on holiday for a week and that she loved them very much. Faith was informed that at the end of her holiday she would receive a suitcase at her hotel to bring back to the States. She laughed as she explained that she didn't even get as far as the airport and was arrested on the way – she was clearly not a seasoned criminal. She then talked about the fear that gripped her as bag after bag of cocaine was removed from the lining of the suitcase – a total of 6 kilograms of cocaine was piled up in front of her. Faith was advised to plead guilty to trafficking drugs and in doing so received a four-year jail sentence. She placed her hand on mine, looked me in the eyes and quietly whispered that she was grateful for the leniency shown by the courts when sentencing her. She was now serving her final year.

Somehow Faith and I found a connection and as the other visitors turned away we continued to talk. I asked Faith what had sustained her over the years. Faith explained that initially, like many prisoners, she had turned to drugs – we both shook our heads at the irony. Two years ago she had rediscovered her faith and it was her faith that was now sustaining her. She explained that on a daily basis she opens the bible to find verses of encouragement. Sometimes she keeps looking until she finds a suitable one. Something in the depths of my subconscious prompted me to smile. Faith immediately asked me to share my thoughts. Somewhat hesitantly I shared my experience in a card shop. I told her that whilst searching for a suitable birthday card I came across one that made me chuckle. A man that was sitting on the roof of a building and flood water was rising all around him. First one boat went past and asked if they could help him. He replied, 'No, I'm waiting for the Lord to rescue me.' As the waters continued to rise a second boat went past and offered to help. But again the man replied, 'No, I'm waiting for the Lord to rescue me.' As the waters reached the roof a helicopter flew past and offered to help but yet again the man replied, 'No, I'm waiting for the Lord to rescue me.' The man died and when he reached the pearly gates he asked, 'Why didn't the Lord rescue me?' He was told that the Lord tried three times. Grace laughed and thanked me but I simply wanted to apologise for recounting something that seemed out of context and irrelevant.

She went on and talked about God's mercy, grace and forgiveness – she had sought and received forgiveness from her God. It was apparent that Faith was at peace with herself. She added that her family was a source of strength and support – her mother was raising her children. Her American lawyer was proactive and was trying to ensure that she could start with a clean slate once back in the States. I didn't understand all the legal complications but in essence what Faith wanted was to do her time and put her crime behind her and not let it label her forever. Faith said she was looking to the future, to being reunited with her children and family and doing something meaningful with her life. I had a strong sense that she would do something purposeful as a result of this journey. I asked Faith if she needed anything. She asked for a blanket and I promised to get her one.

The women persuaded the guards to allow us to see their cells. We made our way through the crowds in the courtyard and up a dark busy staircase. On the way up, I spotted a couple engaged in an energetic mouth to mouth exercise. At the top of the stairs there were long corridors to the right and the left, with cells on either side. A typical cell was the square length of a single bed, with beds criss-crossed three high above each other. The prisoners had few personal possessions. In one cell I noticed a mother with a very young baby and learnt that the prison housed women and children. Faith told me that the capacity of the prison is 250 and presently there are over 500 inmates, 200 of which are children. Some of my fellow visitors seemed paralysed by the feeling of claustrophobia and voiced their desire to leave. In contrast, the prisoners had adapted to the life that they would be living for the forthcoming years. As we were leaving, Faith hugged me tightly and said, 'Thank you for the story,' – perhaps something spoke to her, perhaps her own inner voice had warned her against doing the drugs run. I will never know.

As we exited our arms were checked and passports returned. Most of the visitors were stunned into silence by the experience and initially seemed unable to voice their thoughts and feelings. One young volunteer spent the return trip in tears. What could I do other than listen and allow her to cry? I overheard a number of comments from the other visitors. Some were sympathetic and others condemnatory. I said nothing at the time but now my head is full of many questions. Why do we end up in the situations that we end up in? Are they always of our own making? Why do desperate situations result in equally desperate courses of action for some and not for others? Faith's despair had led to further despair and a black hole of darkness that had swallowed her up. Faith talked about forgiveness. What is forgiveness? Did I see prisoners or people?

Suddenly, the beams from Ben's jeep light up the room and I realise that it had become dark.

***

It is late in the evening and I am lying in bed listening to some music on my MP3 player having just finished my Spanish homework. Not only did I do four hours of lessons today I also had two hours of homework. Over dinner I shared my prison experience with Ben, who kindly listened. Now my mind is once again bombarded with all sorts of issues. I focus on just one – the idea of forgiveness. What is forgiveness and what does it really mean to forgive another person? Who really has the power to forgive? Forgiveness implies wrongdoing. What is wrongdoing and are we all guilty of wrongdoing no matter how great or small? Is there a single person who can claim never to have done wrong and never to have needed forgiveness? Are we in fact a world of wrong doers be it the individual or whole nations? Do we live in a world characterised by wrong doing? Why has society constructed a hierarchy of wrongdoing, where some wrongs are more forgivable than others?

Bugged by all of this, I get out of bed and search the black hole of the Internet for answers. I enter the words, 'Bible, forgiveness', in the Google search engine. I start here as Faith had become a born again Christian.

Matthew 18:21-27 states, ‘Then Peter came to Jesus and asked, ‘Lord, how many times shall I forgive my brother when he sins against me? Up to seven times?’

Jesus answered, ‘I tell you, not seven times, but seventy seven times.’

I then enter the words, ‘Confucius, forgiveness’ and find that Confucius said, ‘Never does a soul appear so strong as when it forgoes revenge and dares to forgive an injury.’

Finally, as a non-practicing Sikh, I note that Guru Nanak said, ‘Where there is forgiveness there is God.’

Sitting at the computer I am fast seeing that forgiveness is integral to the world’s major faiths and philosophies. I discover that even psychologists of the modern world advocate that health and well being are linked with a willingness to forgive – it is important both to forgive and to seek forgiveness.

I hear a noise from Ben’s room and hope that he does not wake up and ask what I’m doing. At this moment in time it would be difficult to explain the ramblings of my brain. I think about modern society and struggle to fit the concept of forgiveness. I question if we live in an unforgiving world, a world focused on retribution, a readiness to judge and condemn and a reticence to understand and show compassion. Phrases that come to mind are, ‘Don’t get mad get even,’ ‘Collateral damage,’ and ‘Zero tolerance,’ and my brain is bombarded by images of revenge and retribution that are all around me. I ask what values drive today’s society but decide not to tackle this question tonight.

Faith and the other prisoners were punished for their crimes and showed remorse. Once they leave prison I hope each of them is allowed to leave their crime behind and not be forever labelled by it. I hope that society will forgive them. However, I fear that society will neither forgive nor forget. I move from the micro or individual wrongdoing to macro wrongdoing and think about the exploitation of poor countries by rich countries and companies and how the creation of poverty and death in the former fuels the wealth in the latter. As an Indian I consider Bhopal where an explosion inside the Union Carbide factory sent 27 tons of methyl isocyanate gas across the shantytowns. Over 20 years later, no one has admitted any wrong doing or sought forgiveness, let alone face criminal charges. When will those who exploit, rape and plunder poorer countries lament and seek forgiveness for their wrongdoing? Why does the very law that punishes individuals, protect those with power and influence?

It is 2am in the morning and time for sleep. However, I know that I will be coming here again. I put the computer to sleep, tiptoe past Ben's room and slip into mine via the chill out room.

Thursday 27th October...

It's lunchtime and I'm back at the Magic Bean café having just completed my second morning of lessons. Whilst sipping a cold freshly squeezed mixed fruit juice I contemplate doing my homework. I look around and notice that two other Europeans already have several study books spread impressively across their tables. I only possess a single A4 course workbook, courtesy of the school, and my Spanish dictionary. At the moment my brain hurts and motivation eludes me. Staring at the textbook I find myself thinking about the English attitude towards learning foreign languages. Why do so many English people expect everyone in the world to speak English and why so often do we utter the phrase, 'Do you speak English?' Why are we so reluctant to learn another language? By refusing to learn another's language, what are we really saying? Are we saying that it is of lesser importance? Surely language goes beyond a means of verbal exchange and communicates one's history, heritage, culture and religion. By learning a language are we not accessing the diverse richness of another country? 80% of people in Ecuador speak Spanish as a first language thanks to the arrival of the Spanish Conquistadors in 1534 and their subsequent rule. With the Spanish came Catholicism and all its influence on the lives of the indigenous population. Despite the Spanish reign, some of the indigenous languages survived and today are spoken by 20% of the population. I ponder my mother tongue and consider how Punjabi is symbolic of the Sikh culture and religion and rooted in Sanskrit. Sanskrit, a five thousand-year-old language, is regarded as the mother of most languages in India and at one time had wide spread influence in Asia and is believed to be the root of most European languages. So rather than saying that Sanskrit is the

Latin of India it would be more appropriate to say that Latin is the Sanskrit of Europe.

***

My thoughts return to lunch as the waiter brings my chips and bread role. So English! As I munch my chip butty, I turn my attention to the regular verb endings and the list of food words that I need to learn for tomorrow's lesson. I realise that learning another language is difficult and having a command of other languages has both its advantages and drawbacks. Knowing some French is helping me to learn the grammar quickly and easily. However, I find myself reverting to French and accessing words that I had assumed were lost in the archives of my memory. I tell myself that the two languages are similar and therefore easy to mix up. Take the phrase, 'I think', which in the French is, 'Je pense,' and in the Spanish, 'Yo pienso.' How similar is that? And words like, 'En,' and, 'Que,' have the same meanings in both languages but are pronounced very differently. Besides, it would be worse if I reverted to Punjabi, as that would really confuse the teacher. Despite rekindling the French I am rapidly learning Spanish. I now know useful phrases like, 'How do you say...in Spanish,' 'I don't speak Spanish but I am learning,' and, 'I don't understand.' I have refrained from learning the phrase, 'Do you speak English?'

Mercedes, who is married with two children, is perplexed by my over keen interest in the grammar. I explained that my engineering background instilled in me the need to deconstruct and then reconstruct in order to understand. She simply raised her eyebrows and smiled at me politely so something must clearly have got lost in the translation. Contrary to the school literature that claimed all its teachers speak good English, I soon realised that Mercedes has a limited command of the language. Frequently I revert to my dictionary to find the meaning of words. I don't mind as she is pleasant enough and I am learning the language. Fingers crossed, I have even avoided drifting off during the lessons. After an hour or so of verbs I take a walk around the area.

Friday 28th October…

It's lunchtime and I am sitting alone in a local restaurant with my homework – it's occupying the seat next to me. This is definitely a locals restaurant, full of locals, eating local food, at local prices. It is a functional restaurant, where you enter, you order, you sit, you eat, you pay and you leave. The standard menu comprises a drink, soup and a main dish. There is no pretence and there are no trimmings. The faded white paint on the walls is flaking. People are sitting around Formica tables on cheap moulded plastic chairs. The tables are lined up on either side of the central entrance with a gap of six inches between each. There's no room for Englishness about personal space. I pretend to blend in by speaking my newly acquired Spanish but the locals aren't fooled. I tell the impatient waiter that I want the chicken. He yells the word, 'Pollo,' across the room in the direction of the kitchen and moves to the next table.

At the end of this morning's lessons, I negotiated doing two hours a day, four days a week. My excuse was that it would allow me more time to digest the learning. In reality, my concentration had let me down and I had drifted off when the teacher was explaining the difference between el pez and el pescado – living fish and dead fish. I imagined that I was sitting in my usual spot and updating the fish on events. I already had so much to tell them. When I heard the words, 'Comprende, comprende,' I returned to the room saying, 'Si, si.'

The tutor was happy with my suggestion providing I did a minimum of three hours homework a day. I'm not sure if overall I was any better off but nodded in agreement.

***

Whilst waiting for my lunch, I decide to read the leaflets that I collected during my stroll yesterday afternoon. I stumbled across an organisation called Ecuador Volunteers and popped in. Twenty minutes later I walked out again having agreed to visit a children's project the following Monday. I was informed that the project works with street children and is located in the old town. If I liked it, I could sign up as a volunteer for a fee of $80. Over dinner at a local Chinese restaurant – the cooker is beyond repair and has been condemned – I chewed over my thoughts with Ben. I could do voluntary work in the mornings, possibly with the children's project, and Spanish lessons in the afternoons. I floated the idea of giving a day a week to Ben's school, the least I could do given that he was putting up with me for free. Ben liked my proposal and agreed to discuss it with the head teacher. He seemed impressed that I wasted no time in sorting out a schedule of activities. Ben talked about next week's half term holiday. Paul and Ximena, a couple that I met at the football last weekend, had proposed spending a few days in Mindo. We would leave on Monday afternoon and return on Wednesday. This fitted perfectly into my own plans except I would need to rearrange all my Spanish lessons. Ben added that he would be away on a rugby tournament in Bogotá from Wednesday until Sunday, the day of his 40th birthday.

I move my leg and feel a sudden twinge of pain. I lift my trousers and sneak a peek at the six-inch oval shaped purple culprit on my right shin. I acquired this last night on the way back from the restaurant whilst greeting a manhole. Ben looked over his shoulder when he heard me yell and then looked down. Satisfied that I was okay, he couldn't stop himself from laughing as he yanked me out. Public safety is not the same as in the UK and cracked pavements, uncovered holes and potholes are the norm. Crossing the roads remains a daily adventure and I'm still learning the rules, if indeed there are any other than not getting knocked down. I'm sure with time I will become acclimatised.

***

I look up as two plates land on the table before me. It's my friendly waiter. I utter the word, 'Perdon,' as I cover my bare leg. As I eat my lunch, which is very tasty, I complete my homework and continue to watch the local life. The face of every person that enters the restaurant confirms that most people have a hard life in this country. After an hour or so, I sense that I have outstayed my welcome at this restaurant. I pay 70 centavos for my vegetable soup, chicken, rice and beans and leave.

Monday 31st October…

It is late in the evening and Ben and I are sitting on the veranda of a wooden hostel in Mindo. The word hostel is a little misleading as it is more like a bed and breakfast type establishment. Mindo itself is a small quaint village located in the cloud forest at an altitude of 1,600 metres and about a 2½ hour drive North West of Quito. The place is a tourist attraction because of its flora, fauna, birds and hill walks. I've just read that a cloud forest is a tropical or sub-tropical mountain forest characterised by a high occurrence of low level cloud cover – I take a moment to digest the imagery. Cloud forests are often found near the peaks of coastal mountains and differ from rainforests in that they are wetter, more lush and cooler.

Surrounded by the sound of humming birds, we are sharing the remains of a beer and chit chatting about nothing in particular. We laugh at the way I ended up meeting some of Ben's rugby friends on Saturday evening. I had turned up at the local restaurant called, 'Dos Argentinos,' and whilst waiting for Ben got talking to two female Europeans. Within minutes they worked out that I was Ben's friend from England and explained he had mentioned that I was coming to Ecuador. They added that they too were waiting for the rugby players. We introduced ourselves and I learnt that Saskia was from Germany and Caz from England. Caz was there with her adopted daughter Jessie, a little Ecuadorian girl. By the time the rugby players turned up there was an impressive collection of empty beer bottles on the table.

In some disconnected way we find ourselves talking about chilling out. I don't tell Ben that I chill out on a daily basis with the pond life. His idea of chilling out at the end of the week is to sit in front of the computer and read the minute by minute football commentary, which is exactly what he did on Saturday. He is a Crystal Palace fan and has calculated the probability of Palace being promoted to the Premiership. A typical mathematician! The football connection leads to a discussion about Sunday's local football match and we agree that it was mediocre. El Nacional played against Aucas and lost 2-4. This game was even worse than last week and two of the goals were comical. I tell Ben that I am left even less convinced by the ability of this team.

Before going to bed we agree to trudge up some hill tomorrow. Neither of us is enticed by the bird watching with its 5am start.

Tuesday 1st November...

Ben and I have just crossed a fast flowing river on a rickety pulley chair and are ambling up some wooded hill in search of a waterfall. The chair certainly would not meet any regulatory standards back in the UK but that did not deter us. You really can acclimatise to different standards. The patches of blue have gradually lost their ground to the Cumulus clouds that are now dominating the skies above. I fear that we are likely to be greeted by rain. The ground is covered with interesting fauna much of which I am unable to name. Paul and Ximena decided not to join us as Ximena is about seven months pregnant. They are planning to get married in December and hopefully before their daughter is born. Paul's parents will shortly be flying out for a three month stay.

***

As I walk I am reliving my introductory visit to the children's project. I turned up at Ecuador Volunteers yesterday morning at 10am. Maria, the representative from the organisation, thought it best to go by public transport and we caught the local bus that took approximately 40 minutes to reach the Place de Santa Domingo in the old town. This experience of local transport was very different from the Ecovia. There was no clearly marked bus stop or clearly marked buses. We stood on the street and when the third bus was about to pass by Maria stuck her hand out and we got on as the bus was still moving. This I deduced was the norm as every few minutes I saw people jump on and off. I took the opportunity to watch the local life through the window and on the bus itself. Several vendors joined the bus to sell their wares, which amongst other things included incense sticks, local papers and candy. My observations were interspersed with bits of information from Maria, which focused on all the dangers. She told me that the area houses ex-prisoners, drug users, prostitutes and alcoholics. It was important to avoid Guayaquil, the street renown for muggings and goodness knows what else, as well as a number of other streets. It was advisable not to carry valuables and not to stay in the area after dark. After hearing the don't's and don't's I knew that surviving the journey to and forth would be challenging. I asked about the project and the children. I learnt that the project is run by nuns and supported by the church. The children come from very deprived families. Many families are simply so poor that they cannot afford to feed their children. Some parents have alcohol and drug related problems and cannot care for their children. A few are going through temporary crisis. Unable to cope, families either bring their children to charitable projects or leave them on the streets where they are picked up by the police.

Once we got off the bus, we had a short walk to the project itself, which ironically was on a street just off Guayaquil. There were two sets of entrance gates leading to the interior of the building. The first was wide open and the second locked. The second set reminded me of the entrance gates to the prison and I had a momentary flashback to my fear but quickly reassured myself that I would not need my passport to enter or exit this facility. Chalked on the left wall between the two gates was the name of the establishment. I only recognised the word, 'Jesus.' A young woman in her teens opened the second gate and greeted us with a smile. As we entered I noticed a staircase to the left and just ahead an open courtyard approximately 80m square. In the courtyard to my left were a group of children dressed in brown overalls. They were all varnishing bits of wood with a very strong smelling reddish/brown varnish and their fingers and hands were as stained as the wood. I estimated that their ages ranged from 7 to 14 years. Most of them said, 'Hola.' I was told that the children were learning carpentry and producing wooden puzzles that would be sold to raise funds for the project. Above to my right, back, and left were balconies that led into a number of rooms. At the far end of this concrete courtyard was another gate that led to a smaller courtyard and to the left of this gate was an office. My first encounter with a nun was in this small office when I was cornered, had a sheet of paper thrust into my hand and was talked at for several minutes. When the scary sister, did bother to take a breath, perhaps in anticipation for an answer to some question that she had posed I simply said, 'No hablo Español y no entiendo.'

I had communicated this effectively as she turned to Maria and asked where I was from. When told England she looked at the colour of my skin and raised her eyebrows. I considered being humorous and saying, 'It's just a bloody good sun tan,' but such frivolity was suppressed by a grin. Anyway, the humour might have been lost in translation. Maria informed me that the sheet of paper was nothing important, just the rules and code of conduct that volunteers were expected to abide by. Unable to read the Spanish I decided that I would make up my own rules and returned the paper to the nun with a big smile. Two minutes with the nun and the devil inside of me had already grown a hundred-fold and I was doing my best to keep her from making a public appearance. I knew there and then that I would be working here.

At the end of the second courtyard was the kitchen and the dining room and to the left a concrete staircase that led to the two lower floors. On the first were the classrooms, two offices, and the girls' dormitory. Lower down were toilets and another courtyard which was the children's play area – 60 square metres of concrete. There were no play structures and no toys. I spotted two burst footballs. To the left of this courtyard, was a long concrete sink above which hung several washing lines full of clothes. An external metal staircase led to the boys' dormitory. After this brief guided tour Maria took me to the classrooms to meet the other volunteers, more children and the teacher. Five adults, 8 children and now two visitors were crammed into one small room even though there were two larger rooms running off this room. One adult whom I guessed was the teacher was attempting to teach the vowels by asking the children to chant, a, e, i, o, u. One or two feigned interest but the rest just moved about randomly in the tight space. Her constant shouting and threats to use violence had little impact. My initial impression was that the theory of chaos would be challenged in this setting. Maria suggested that I could help support the classroom work as education was important.

The children were of varying ages and abilities, unkempt and suffering from malnutrition. Several came and hugged me, whether I wanted to be hugged or not, and one wrapped his limbs around me like the tentacles of an octopus and I needed help to peel him off. One of the girls that had an immediate impact on me was a disabled girl called Julia. No one knew her precise age or the nature of her disability, other than she had no speech. So I was at home as neither of us could communicate verbally in a common language. She grabbed me by the hand, took me to where she was sitting, vacated the seat to her right by shoving the child off it and pointed me to it. I obliged by sitting down next to her. She then pinched a well chewed pencil from the child on her left, forced it in my hand and pointed to a piece of paper and grinned. Her face lit up and disclosed a real cheekiness. The grin also revealed a missing front tooth and teeth that were in urgent need of treatment. I watched her closely and noted that when other children tried to get my attention she soon dissuaded them in her own way. I was her friend only and not to be shared. Despite this behaviour, the other children were very protective and caring towards her. I could not help but think who needs verbal communication? Two boys, Michael and Jacson without the k also made an impression. Michael aged about 8 years presented with a physical disability and some delayed speech. He seemed a cheeky child who enjoyed getting into mischief and not doing as he was told. Jacson, no more than 9 years of age, was of African descent. He had a limited concentration span and needed a lot of attention. These two were good friends and I sensed that together could be double trouble. The four volunteers who were in their late teens and twenties seemed lost in the chaos but were very caring towards the children. Only one volunteer – a French woman – looked as if she did not want to be there. I concluded that she would not last. Interestingly, the children had sensed this and did not interact with her. When we were about to leave, Julia decided that I was not going anywhere and used the half Nelson to wrestle me back onto the chair that I hardly lifted myself out off. She let go when I said that I'll be back and waved as I left the room. I heard the teacher say that she didn't understand anything. Let's not enlighten her I told myself.

As we left the building and headed for the bus, I noticed the statue of the Virgin Mary on top of the hill. She was looking down on the area with her arms open wide. I remembered that I had walked to the top of that hill, called, 'El Panecillo,' on my last trip and that the statue was called, 'La Virgen de Quito.' I spotted some prostitutes on a street corner within a few feet of the police. Both groups went about their business and appeared to co-exist in a strange harmony.

The return journey was less pleasurable as I had the opportunity to receive free insults from the local religious drunk. It was a big mistake to sit on the back row facing the centre isle as there was nothing to hide behind and the drunk had my undivided attention. Without speaking a word of Spanish, I knew that he was not saying, 'And blessings I bestow upon you.' Maria commented that it was not the best place to sit. I wanted to say that I knew that already but silence seemed a better option. A smile was brought to my face as the bus braked very suddenly and the chap went flying down the isle. I immediately reprimanded myself for smiling at his misfortune. This experience was enough to deter me from using public transport. On the way back Maria explained that her organisation was having problems with the project and in particular with Sister T and that I could choose a different project if I wanted to. I responded by saying that I could start on Thursday and do four mornings a week for the next two months. I was tempted to add that I liked a challenge but kept the thought to myself.

***

I suddenly reach a junction in the woods and turn to Ben who I realise is about twenty feet behind. When he catches up we pick a route up the hill. As we continue walking we talk about our mutual interests other than walking and sports. We discover that we both like playing scrabble. Ben announces that he can beat me and in doing so throws down the gauntlet. We agree to borrow Paul's travel scrabble next week to find out who is the better player.

Eventually we reach the metal gate that leads to the waterfall and pay five bucks each to enter. The little man operating the gate leads us down a steep slippery path, which in places is very vertiginous and not for the fainthearted. At the edge of a sheer 100-foot drop he tells us that it is the route to the waterfall. As Ben and I turn to each other to check that we hadn't misinterpreted the Spanish, the guy points out the vertical ladder attached precariously to the rock face and starts walking away. Ben says thanks to the bloke's back. Leaving the big rucksack behind we descend down the ladder to the edge of the river. We continue walking and stop in the middle of a bouncy footbridge – which is even bouncier as I find myself treating it like a trampoline – to get a good view of the waterfall. We are both dumbstruck with disbelief as we stare at the trickle of water – had someone turned off the tap? Unexcited by the sight we continue strolling down the river. The afternoon rain makes its appearance so we stop under some trees for a lunch of dried fruit, chocolate and water. As the rain looks comfortably settled in for the remainder of the day, we turn back and retrace our steps to the Butterfly Centre to meet the others. On the way back we entertain the possibility of tackling Cotopaxi at Christmas, just the kind of thing that one does whilst meandering lazily through the woods. At a mere 5,897 metres above sea level, Cotopaxi is Ecuador's highest active volcano.

Over dinner the four of us speak in a combination of English, Spanish and French. Ximena only speaks French and Spanish and I retrieve even more of my French from the recesses of my brain and for every new Spanish word I am recovering a French word. I find myself liking Ximena very much – intuitively we are on the same wavelength – and I feel frustrated at my inability to speak Spanish. We all agree to have a leisurely breakfast whilst bird watching from the comfort of the hostel veranda and to stop at the Pululahua volcanic crater on the way back providing the weather is clear. The crater is at an elevation of 3,356 m and on a clear day offers spectacular views of farms and forests. We vote against the touristy Mitad del Mundo – middle of the world – where the Equator allegedly divides the Northern and Southern Hemispheres.

Thursday 3rd November...

It is only 6.30am and I am awake. It could be the sheer excitement of the voluntary work that I will be starting in a few hours time or, more likely, the fact that I set my alarm an hour earlier than intended. Whilst persuading my limbs to take action, I'm wondering what to do with my unexpected free afternoons. I cancelled my Spanish lessons for the first three days of the week but had arranged lessons for Thursday and Friday. However, yesterday I received an e-mail informing me that the school would be closed due to the public holiday. Ximena told me that this public holiday, called the, 'Dia de los Muertos,' or the, 'Day of the Dead,' is a time when dead family members are remembered. She explained that November 2nd is the official date for the Day of the Dead and families visit the graves of their loved ones and adorn them with flowers. As she spoke, my mind was finding its own unique way of receiving this information. The name alone was sufficient to trigger clips from films like, '28 Days Later,' and, 'Shaun of the Dead.' I visualised Zombies – brought back to life by a curse or ritual – coming out of graves, feasting on fresh human meat, drinking beer and having a right laugh by causing chaos in cities and towns all over Ecuador. I didn't share my personal amusement with any of my new friends. Yesterday, I discovered that the Day of the Dead is in fact a time of celebration. I witnessed first hand the fiesta whilst caught in traffic on the way back from Mindo. The streets were full of vendors and people who were all dressed up. Vendors were selling breads, flowers, candles, incense sticks, paper puppets and all sorts of food. As we drove past one cemetery we came to a crawl, as the cars ahead were slowly squeezing past cars parked on every bit of pavement. Here I saw hundreds of people walking into the cemetery carrying flowers that looked like Marigolds. There was a colourful party atmosphere and I imagined decaying corpses and the living having a dead good party in broad daylight and each returning to their respective homes by nightfall. Lying here I entertain the idea of a day for the living dead, a day to help those who still walk the planet to become alive again.

***

Looking around my room, my bags are now unpacked, I spot the art materials on the shelving unit. Maybe I will do some sketching over the next few days. It's a possibility amongst so many. My need for caffeine and the bathroom cause me to get out of bed. I top up the kettle with bottled water, turn it on and head towards the bathroom. The only drawback of this square-shaped tiled bathroom is that there is no bath. I switch on the shower and as I am about to step in I notice the blue sky and in the yonder distance the almost perfect cone-like shape of Cotopaxi. So Ben wasn't winding me up after all. Perhaps I could sketch Ben using the photograph that I took in Mindo. Getting up early has allowed me to enjoy a leisurely breakfast of Cornflakes and fruit. Over breakfast I think about my first day as a volunteer and study the A3 map of the old town. Ben again has sorted this out for me. Although I am not walking up a mountain, I choose to wear my dark walking trousers, dark top, fleece and trainers. I'm selecting clothes that are quick to wash and dry. After my bus experience I had decided that I would travel to and from the project by taxi, using the taxis at the taxi rank on Madrid. At times we all need a comfort blanket and a door to door taxi would be mine. At 8.20am I grab my keys, which I hide in an internal zipped pocket, five dollars, the map and a small bottle of water. All the way to Madrid I am practising my key phrases, 'Buenos dias señor,' – good morning, 'Calle Guayaquil, circa de Place de Santa Domingo' – Guayaquil near Place de Santa Domingo, and, 'Perdon, cuánta cuesta?' – How much will it cost?

***

I have just returned home from my first day at work and by a mere two minutes have avoided getting absolutely drenched by the usual afternoon downpour. From the dryness of the living room I watch the monsoon style rain bouncing three inches off the front patio. Once again I eye the flower bed that would certainly make a damn fine fish pond. I could make it my weekend project and surprise Ben when he returns on Sunday. I guess it would be one hell of a birthday surprise. A cup of Yorkshire tea beckons especially after the beer that I have just consumed with Iki. A beer in the afternoon really doesn't suit my metabolism and I want to fall asleep. However, my itchy scalp triggers me into action, a shower and a change of clothes. Tucked in a sleeping bag on the sofa and mug of tea in hand I find myself scratching my head. I know that this is purely psychological so I pull my hand away and tell myself that I have not caught nits on my first day as a volunteer.

Talking about my first day, I turned up at 8.45am following an easy taxi ride thanks to my fluent Spanish. Well actually the ability to point to the map and show an address interspersed with good morning, thank you and I am from England did the trick. When I arrived at the project I discovered that no one was expecting me so I made my way to the racket that was emanating from the dining room. Sister T, or rather, Scary Nun as I renamed her after my first encounter, was not about. Julia recognised me straight away but an invisible ball and chain stopped her from leaving her seat and coming over. However, nothing could stop her from smiling. I immediately gathered that the children had to remain seated until they finished eating. Every few moments the teacher was telling them to be quiet – the word, 'Ssh,' needed no translation. The children were sitting in groups of four around square wooden tables and eating their breakfast of what can only be described as gruel. I suddenly thought about Oliver Twist and decided that no child would be saying, 'Please sir, can I have some more?' There was no more and there was no Oliver here. I spotted Iki, the female volunteer that I met on my introductory visit. Her first words to me were, 'It's crazy here,' followed by, 'Hello,' and, 'Sit next to me.'

As soon as I sat down I received the evil eye from the teacher and simply responded with a smile. Seated on a wooden stool, I watched as each child finished their breakfast and washed their dishes in cold water in the long narrow white sink. After a few minutes Iki asked me to join her in the classroom as she wanted to share her experience – all four days worth to be precise. She explained that children who were not funded to attend school remained in the building and did carpentry or nothing. With fire and passion she told me that the carpentry was little more than free labour and the children were not actually learning any carpentry skills – they spent all day polishing the pre-cut wooden pieces. She did not take to the nuns or the teacher. The teacher had taught nothing but the vowels. She had no educational programme in place and since the arrival of the volunteers had retreated to her office to read the paper. The angrier Iki became the faster she spoke. There were no educational resources. Consequently, she and the other volunteers had spent their own money buying books, pencils and other resources. Only three of the four volunteers that I met on my first visit remained – the French woman had quit. The young German lad called Michael was told to do carpentry with the children and the other lad only worked in the afternoons. Iki was left to teach the children on her own. She had tried to work with the children in two groups; the younger ones between 9.00 and 10.30 and the older ones from 10.30 until 12 when lunch was served. My only comment was, 'Wow.'

My first suggestion was to use the larger classroom. This room consisted of old small wooden tables and chairs suitable for young children only – all were in a bad state and needed to be thrown out. On one wall there was a decent sized marker board, but the other two walls and low level wooden partition wall were bare. The only source of natural light was from the high horizontal windows on one of the external walls. There was no positive feel to the room as a classroom, no sense that it was a place where children's learning had been encouraged and achievements celebrated. I found that sound echoed badly off the tall ceiling. But we had to make do with what we had.

The first group of nine children aged 2 to 10 years arrived at 9.05. It included my friend Julia and the inseparable Michael and Jacson. It was no surprise that these two sat next to each other and butted the edges of their tables together. On seeing the children, I proposed using the session to assess each child's ability and to differentiate them accordingly. We set up play activities for Julia and the 2 year old. Play activities is not the correct term as the only toys we found were a box of plastic farm animals. For the rest we provided colouring pencils and pictures to colour whilst asking them to identify the alphabet and numbers. This was a bit difficult as the children had to share one pencil case of colouring pencils. Despite these limitations we noted that some had poor or no pencil control. We discovered that the concentration of all the children was limited and concluded that we would need to plan a range of activities and run each for a short period of time. None of the children could read or write so it was a case of starting from scratch. We decided to start by teaching the alphabet, beyond the vowels and numbers up to 20. Our work was cut out for us but even I could contribute on my first day as I had been taught the alphabet. Talk about being one step ahead of the kids. They were perplexed and asked why I knew the alphabet but could speak only a few words. Disbelievingly, Jacson kept asking, 'No habla Español?'

And I kept replying, 'No hablo.'

Both Michael and Jacson were well behaved but both they and I knew that it wouldn't last. Julia was not amused that my attention had to be shared with the other children and every five minutes I had to sit with her for two and just give her praise for the lines she had scribbled onto an A4 sheet of paper. At 10.15 the children asked for a story and selected one from the collection of four that Iki had found in the office. They chose, 'El Patito Feo,' – The Ugly Duckling. You didn't need a degree in psychology to understand the significance of their choice. Listening to stories was a new experience for most of the children and they all packed tightly around Iki and were totally absorbed by the story. Julia had pulled up two chairs making her expectations crystal clear and I duly obliged.

The second group turned up at 10.30 and kicked the remaining children from the first group out of the room. This group of five girls was aged 9 to 14 years and again of mixed ability. Four girls had some command of literacy and numeracy but the 14 year old Heidi could only write her name. This was due to the effort invested by Iki in her first three days. Before this week Heidi could not write her name but now wrote it repeatedly with pride. She was so proud of her achievements that as she walked into the room she snatched the black marker pen from my hand and wrote her name on the board. Heidi was the only other child of African descent. I worked with Heidi on the alphabet whilst Iki worked with the other girls. This session was only interrupted every 20 minutes by Julia who kept sticking her head around the door and grinning manically. Iki looked at me as if to say, you tell her off, so I walked up to her and said 'Mañana mi amiga.' Julia thought it was a really great game and I just thought, 'Whatever,' and played along.

At 12 noon we dismissed the children and decorated the plain walls with their work and greatly improved the appearance of the room. I decided that there would be no bare wall by Christmas and every child would have their work displayed. Iki asked if I could stay until 2pm as it was shower day and the disabled girls needed help. I agreed as I had no Spanish classes. However, the next priority was lunch.

Over a lunch of pizza and chips we exchanged some personal details. Iki told me that she is Swiss French with Spanish heritage from her father's side. This explained her command of Spanish and French – speaking some English seems to be a given for most Europeans. She was coming to the end of a world wide trip that she had undertaken with her boyfriend. In Ecuador, she decided to do four weeks of voluntary work whilst her boyfriend studied Spanish – she had never worked with children before. She explained that she will shortly be 26 and wanted to celebrate her birthday with the children. She wanted to buy the children gifts and a cake. I said that it was a very kind idea. I found Iki to be as volatile as the surrounding volcanic mountains but I liked her fiery spirit and knew we would work well together. I observed that like me she was a slim build but a couple of inches shorter at 5ft 2". Iki advised that I buy a head scarf like hers to reduce the risk of getting nits from the children and to treat my head once a week with nit lotion. So the head scarf wasn't an unfortunate fashion statement. She deduced that I was English with an Indian heritage – this was a relief as some tourists were mistaking me for a local.

My mountain climb of an education continued into the afternoon, so wearing walking gear was symbolic after all. The girls' dormitory had a total of 14 single beds jutting out from the walls of a square high ceilinged room. The bedding consisted of a sheet and blanket. Some had pillows and many didn't. All the walls were painted brilliant white. Even the floor had shiny white tiles. Like the classroom the only natural light was from the horizontal windows on one external wall. The girls had few personal effects and most of them had only one change of clothes that was kept in an open shelving unit just outside the dormitory next to the sick room. They shared a single bathroom comprising a shower, a toilet without a toilet seat and a wash basin. In here I noticed a dirty black bucket containing their toothbrushes and on the sink a single dark green bar of soap. There was no toothpaste.

We helped the girls to shower and washed their hair using the soap because there was no shampoo. Iki told me that they had to shower in their underwear which was some religious expectation. The nuns did not explain such things as periods. This was left to the teenager who lived at the project with the girls. Sex and sexuality were taboo subjects. I wondered at what age they would be issued their chastity belts. After the showers, we combed and plaited the girls' long dark hair and used elastic bands to tie the ends of the plaits. We took turns to share the one comb. I knew that whilst the girls were sharing this one comb the nits would continue to reign. The girls' hair was similar to my own, black and thick. Unlike mine, theirs felt like straw. I wanted to get rid of the nits and then treat their hair with warm oil to restore the softness – just like my mother used to do with mine when I was a child. I couldn't even brush Heidi's hair as I needed a wide tooth comb. I could see that it desperately needed some specialist attention.

Iki had invested in a huge bottle of moisturising lotion and the girls used this on their dry hands and faces. Given Julia's disability I creamed both her hands and face. The white on her nails revealed a calcium deficiency. As I finished she stuck out her arms so I creamed them as well. This resulted in a queue of girls all wanting their arms moisturised. As we both creamed away, we knew that what they really wanted and needed was a motherly touch. Watching the girls, it was clear to me that in the absence of a motherly figure they nurtured each other. Those who had been nurtured were nurturing those who needed it. The older ones took responsibility for the well being of the younger ones. Wet and tired we departed just after 2pm. We headed to the Place de Santa Domingo where Iki introduced me to the Trole bus service, a tram service that stopped at specified locations along the Avenida de 10 de Agosto. We stopped in Mariscal and went for a coffee at the Coffee House café. That was the plan but instead we opted for beers. Well it was a hard day at work. After the beers and a chat I headed up the hill back to La Floresta.

***

It's now 5.30pm. The rain has stopped so I decide to pop out for some water as I am running low. I head up the hill to the corner shop and buy a five litre bottle of water and a spicy chicken pasty as I fancy something hot. I return to the house and enjoy the pasty whilst sitting in front of the computer. Instead of reading and responding to e-mails I am distracted by a web search. I heard the word, 'Mestizos,' in reference to the children today and want to know its meaning. I discover that approximately 65% of the population in the country is Mestizo or of mixed racial ancestry, which in this case is European (Spanish) and Indigenous. 25% of the population is Indigenous and comprises 13 different groups that inhabit different rural regions of the country. Apparently it is possible to distinguish the groups by their clothing. 7% is European and 3% African Ecuadorian. There are only a small number of people of Asian descent which could explain why I have not seen any fellow Indians.

By reading this information I am able to add more detail to the various people that I have encountered so far. The little man that sells the newspaper in the mornings and oranges or mangoes in the afternoon on the central reservation on Toledo is clearly Mestizo. The woman with the baby selling sweets on the corner of 12 de Octubre and Jorge Washington is indigenous. She has classic features and wears traditional dress. I laugh as the other day I walked straight past Jorge Washington as this my human land feature was not there. I later found that she had taken up residence on a street corner on Madrid. I was pleased to see her again as I had got into the habit of greeting her daily and had decided to buy sweets from her once a week to leave with the cleaning money for Gladys. The two middle aged women that occupy the steps of the entrance to the university are Mestizo. They are only there in the mornings and usually sit opposite each other across the steps. I still don't know if they sit there to beg off students or if they work as cleaners at the university.

Most of the children at the project belong to the first group except the two African Ecuadorians. There are no European or Indigenous children or staff.

So far I've seen the biggest concentration of European Ecuadorians in the expensive malls and can guess which group is the wealthiest. After my first working day my head is crammed full. Essential words and phrases including sit down now, wait one moment please, later, tomorrow, very good and well done are competing with everything that I have experienced today. I am too tired to dissect, analyse and reflect so opt to respond to my e-mails, revise the essential words for the morning and surrender my brain to TV junk including a dubbed episode of CSI.

Friday 4th November...

Having survived my second day, Iki and I are now conducting a post mortem on today's events over beer. We bumped into each other just outside the gate at 9am as I was getting out of my comfort mobile and walked into the building to find both children and adults running around like headless lamas. We soon discovered from Michael that the staff had refused to serve breakfast until the kitchen broom had been found and that the children had spent the last half hour searching for it. He added, 'It's crazy here.'

'From everyone's behaviour you could wrongly deduce that we were in the midst of a catastrophic crisis,' I replied and remembered that English was Michael's second language when he looked at me blankly. I told him to ignore me and asked him what brought him to Ecuador. During a further five minutes of chaos I gathered that Michael is 19 years old and came to Ecuador to play in the youth orchestra. His plan is to learn Spanish and do voluntary work for a year and then return to Germany to study medicine. He was excluded from military service because a part of his finger was severed when he was a child. I didn't ask if it was the trigger finger. The project provides his board and lodging and he takes all his meals with the children. He was in the process of telling me that he had lost weight when Scary Nun came marching towards us wagging her finger.

'She is a little scary,' Michael commented.

'Yep,' I replied whilst chuckling.

Fortunately, she was diverted in the direction of the kitchen by someone waving a broom. A kitchen broom or a witch's broom I thought to myself. As volunteers we took the opportunity to make our escape. Michael walked off towards the carpentry but doubled back when he remembered he had to have his breakfast.

Iki and I went off to the lower echelons. We decided to arrange the desks and chairs in accordance with ability. We put the two year old, who I was told is called Henry and belongs to the cook, with Julia as both could get on with some colouring and cutting and gluing. We grouped the three boys aged seven to nine together. We wanted to try and teach Jairo, the 7 year old, with Michael and Jacson. The other four, aged between 5 and 6 years, we decided to seat together and let them develop pencil control skills by going over letters and numbers. Nine children turned up at 9.30am but only seven of the ones from yesterday. Conveniently the teacher popped into the room and sensibly I asked her through Iki what happened to the two children and if it would be possible to have more information about each of the children. She told us that two had gone home and the new child José had turned up during the night. The other child, a disabled girl called Antonia, was not needed in carpentry so we had to have her. As she was leaving the room she eyed the work on the wall and murmured that there was no more information. José told us that he turned 14 this year, which was difficult to believe as he was only 5ft, and that he could read and write. We confirmed the latter for ourselves and asked him to return with the other group at 10.30am. We sat Antonia with the 5 to 6 year olds. Although she tried to communicate it was difficult to decipher the words. She repeatedly drew small neat spirals and was not able to or did not want to trace over the alphabet. Whereas Julia was protected by the other children, Antonia tended to be picked on but demonstrated a real resilience. Overall the arrangement generated a calm environment and facilitated teaching and learning. Jacson wanted to draw and initially refused to learn the alphabet. Not surprisingly, Michael did the same. We agreed that they could both draw next week if they worked today. We covered the alphabet and introduced some basic words. We revised the numbers to 20 and read the same story twice. The story was El Patito Feo.

The second group was a delight, as we had five able kids with whom we could make progress. I learnt three more names; Maria, Myra and Isabel and found out a little more about each of the children. Maria is Jairo's sister. Isabel had broken her ankle whilst trying to escape from the project – she reminded me of Steve McQueen in the film The Great Escape and I knew that she would try again as soon as she could. This snippet of information was offered by the other children as we walked up the stairs at the end of the class. The forth girl's name still eludes me but one of the six year olds in the first group is her younger sister. I only worked with Heidi for 20 minutes as she did not turn up until 11.40am. This was actually useful as Julia kept coming into the room. Ultimately I decided it was easier to just let her sit down and to do some colouring with her, as Iki was coping well with the others. When we asked Heidi for an explanation we learnt that she does all the cleaning in the kitchen and dining room and can only leave when the work is done. She is the only child who is treated in this way. Iki said it was racism. She was livid and ready to quit so I advised not working in the afternoon and chilling out instead – besides how would I have coped without a Spanish speaker.

That is the reason for these afternoon beers. I don't like beer but the wine is expensive and horrid. I share my thoughts with Iki. I suggest that we accept that we cannot change the working context; the way the place is managed, the way the volunteers are treated, and to a certain extent the way the children are treated. However, if we acknowledge that the working conditions will be difficult but keep the focus on the children we will survive and make a difference even if it's only for a short period of time. If we plan carefully we can hand over an established work programme to future volunteers. I add that we need to bear in mind our own limitations, especially in relation to the disabled children who need specialist care. Iki accepts my suggestions. After an hour long discussion we are in a better frame of mind to plan next week's work. We decide that it would be good to let the younger group have a break and play outside for 10 minutes. We agree that it is important to continue teaching mathematics to the older children as well as geography. Reluctantly I offer to give spelling tests to the older children to increase their vocabulary and improve their spelling – Iki believes it to be a good idea as it will increase my confidence to speak the language. We divide up the tasks for next week. I will learn a list of words for Monday's spelling test and buy some story books. Iki will prepare some teaching resources. It's late in the afternoon and we go our separate ways.

Saturday 5th November...

It's 9.00am in the morning. The glorious blue sky is interspersed with Bart Simpson clouds, the sun is shining and Cotopaxi is standing proud in the far distance. I am a woman on a mission. The first is to buy resources for the project and the second is to learn more about the country. Walking up and down the streets in Mariscal, I eventually find a local bookshop. Here, I buy some story books namely, Sleeping Beauty, Pinocchio, the Enchanted Castle and Beauty and the Beast and by doing so double the total number of books at the project. I spend $20 but will take this out of the $80 that I still need to pay to Ecuador Volunteers. I am left with $10. Satisfied with my purchases, I head towards the National Museum to augment my historical awareness. My entrance fee allows me access to the Archaeological Museum and the Modern Art Museum.

The Archaeological Museum, as the name suggests, is full of excavated bits of interesting pottery, ceramic figurines, scary masks, ornaments of gold, silver and platinum, jewellery made from precious and semi-precious stones and other artefacts. All are quaintly displayed in sparklingly clean glass cabinets. It is possible to read about the different groups of people linked to the collections in both Spanish and English. I study the Spanish to see if from the words and phrases I can make out what the information is trying to convey. This adds a bit of interest to the monotony of gleaming glass cabinet after gleaming glass cabinet. I can understand why children find museums so boring. This place is like a morgue; the remains of the dead within a deadly setting. I learn about the pre-Incas, the Incas and the post-Incas (the Spanish). I visualise a new section in 100 years time that will depict the exploits of the present day invaders. The scary masks hasten my exit to the upper level where I enjoy an uninterrupted viewing of 19th and 20th century art work by South

American artists. I am drawn to the pencil work and appreciate how each stroke portrays every physical feature and captures the sitter's mood. I wonder if the sitter could ever have envisaged living so vividly beyond their physical years. I acknowledge that next to these my own work would look pitiful but I am inspired to dust down my graphic sketching pencils.

***

Leaving the museum, I stroll over to Parque El Ejido. The previous Saturday, Ben and I had a whistle-stop tour here between the heavy showers. I bought him a hammock for his birthday. It was time the hooks in the chill out room were put to good use. Today, at a leisurely pace, I enjoy the good weather and study the art produced by local artists. Some of the art work is exceptional and I would gladly part with my money but much of it is poorly executed, repetitive and uninteresting. I visit the stalls that are selling a range of memorabilia to tourists. There are hand-knitted woollens, bags, hats and other clothes as well as arts and crafts. Many of the vendors are indigenous and at several stalls I stand and watch women knitting woollen garments. I am tempted to buy a hat that a woman has just finished but resist. I'm pleased that no one is using any hard sales tactics and fortunately phrases like, 'Have a butchers,' and, 'Cheaper than Asda,' that abound in bazaars across the world have not reached these parts. The bartering is almost as entertaining as in India. It is possible to distinguish seasoned travellers from non-seasoned travellers by what they pay for the merchandise. At one stall, I watch an American tourist pay $35 for two water colours. The locals catch me smiling and shaking my head. I greet them and move on.

After an hour or so I need a rest and claim the centre seat on a set of three rusty old swings from where I absorb life whilst rocking gently. The play facilities comprise swings and an old climbing frame that have outlived their usefulness. Not surprisingly, children are playing everywhere except in the play area. I look around and notice that lots of locals are sitting on the grass in small groups; troublesome teens are mucking about, couples are canoodling and families are enjoying their picnics. Groups of men are seated on the few benches that are dotted around the park. The atmosphere is relaxed and everyone is enjoying the day. In contrast the poor and disabled are roaming and begging off tourists and locals. I cannot imagine when some of these individuals last had a meal, a shower, a change of clothing or a bed for the night. Begging seems to be an accepted way of life in Quito and probably in Ecuador if the information provided by my fellow flight passenger is reliable.

In my walks around the city I have noticed the different ways in which the poorest deal with their poverty. Many have surrendered to the grip of poverty and lie in doorways and streets with minds obliterated by drugs and cheap alcohol. Some walk the streets in a daze offering their open hands to passers-by or wander in and out of tourist restaurants. Others occupy their regular begging spots on a daily basis and are as permanent as the inanimate features that surround them. The central reservations on dual carriageways near to the traffic lights are particularly popular. Some of the poor provide entertainment at these junctions in exchange for a few centavos and I have witnessed some impressive acrobatics and juggling. It is at these junctions that I have seen the largest number of African Ecuadorians – other than on the football pitch. Rather than begging or entertaining many sell small items, such as fruit, sweets, bottled water or the local newspapers. Others offer to wash windscreens. Occasionally drivers do buy items or give money but more often they keep their doors locked and hide behind their tinted windows.

Here in the park, I see that tourists and locals are equally immune to the cries for help and the beggars remain invisible to the naked eye. Why are people reacting in the way that they are? Are they even aware of their own behaviour? Do they even care? How should people respond to these poor people? Should they feel any responsibility? Who is responsible for their plight? My eyes follow the ice-cream vendor who has just completed a third circuit of the park. He stops near the exit and chats to a vendor selling freshly cooked food. The sight triggers my hunger and forces me to leave the park in search of food. My stomach is no more acclimatised against the effects of street food here than it would be in London and I resist all temptation of eating al fresco. On the way out, I notice the beggars that are strategically positioned to beg off tourists and locals entering and leaving the park.

Standing here is a good move as they are likely to encounter all the rich tourists coming across from the Hilton. Walking along the 6 de Deciembre, I find a place called Texas Chicken which amazingly is full of locals. I order by pointing to a picture menu, pay $2 and sit down at a table. A waiter brings my meal of rice, chicken and beans on a tray along with a knife, fork and a single disposable plastic glove. Sneakily, my eyes scan the restaurant to ascertain the purpose of the glove. I discover that customers wear the glove to pick the meat of the chicken so I decide to do the same. I enjoy the meal but leave the inclusive indescribable strawberry coloured fizzy drink untouched.

It's now quite late in the afternoon and I decide to be sensible in respect of my own safety and return home before dark. As the daytime businesses conclude the evening businessmen and women are just starting to display their wares. I walk up Mariscal Foch and find that the women become men dressed up as women and just ahead of me business discussions are being held with the driver of a very expensive car. I cross to the other side of the road before continuing up to 12 de Octubre. Should I have returned a bit earlier? There is always a fine line between personal safety and paranoia. The SAE distribute a safety leaflet which provides useful tips and advice. It's probably best read a few days after one's arrival in the country to resist catching the next return flight home. The section on drugging is especially frightening and reads, 'This involves the use of Scopolamine, better known as the date-rape drug. This drug originates from a plant that grows naturally in the jungle regions of the Andean countries. The drug is colourless and odourless and can be prepared for consumption, inhalation or as a powder that gets absorbed by the skin. Upon ingestion, the victim loses the ability to think clearly and may pass out, making him/her vulnerable to theft or worse. Most frequently, it is slipped into drinks. However, there have been cases of thieves putting it on pamphlets or fliers they hand out on the streets or inviting people to smell perfumes or flowers laced with it. Watch out for people trying to give you anything that you don't ask for. Don't accept any street fliers, already open drinks, or an invitation to buy you a drink from the bar, cigarettes or agree to smell anything! Don't leave your drink unattended, especially in bars or nightclubs!'

Another section talks about opportunistic theft and reads, 'This may seem obvious, but most theft is of an opportunistic nature. Limit this by walking around with valuable items hidden, i.e. wallets, cameras, etc.'

The group of Americans that I spotted this morning with expensive cameras festooned around their necks clearly wanted to donate their possessions to the poor. Perhaps to some the obvious is not so obvious. Ben's wallet was stolen on a crowded bus the week before I arrived and recently a fellow student had his bag snatched at knife point. Sensibly, I carry only $5 dollars except when more is needed, leave my credit cards at home and only withdraw money when out with Ben. I guess people's assumption that all tourists are white maybe a personal advantage.

***

Safely back at home, I download the pictures that I took in Mindo from my Minolta digital camera onto Ben's computer. Armed with my graphic pencils and the new sketch book that I brought with me from England I am ready for the creative battle. Comfortably seated I click a button and fill the screen with Ben's face. As I struggle to get going I realise that the victims of my pencil portraits are usually people that I know well and I find it easy to capture their physical features and convey aspects of their personalities. I once captured Dom in a state of stress using charcoal – I keep promising to give it to him. One of my favourites is that of my oldest friend Muriel, whom I have known since my teens. I sketched it when she reached the golden age of 80 and captured every physical feature and conveyed aspects of her personality – every wrinkle and line tells its own magical story. I would want to be like Muriel when I'm old – a person who is still excited by life, who still enjoys life and who has lived life to the full. I would still want to take a moment to enjoy the inspiration provided by the spring blossom or the sunset at the close of the day. Just like her, I would want to say, 'I'm tired with a capital K.' I would want to be as individual as she is and put it down to, 'Old age and decrepitude,' – as she does. I would want to mirror her humbleness. Maybe I will wear purple as well. I am reminded of the poem entitled, 'Warnings,' by Jenny Joseph and pull it up from the internet.

For me this poem speaks of a woman who wants to be her own person and quite frankly not give a damn about what people might expect or say. Every time I read this poem I chuckle but can't help but think why wait until you are old. Why not live now as you want to live? Or is this a thought too far? Aspects of this poem remind me of Muriel. She wears purple and deserves a PhD in the art of hoarding. Her idea of tidying is to take things from one place and put them somewhere else – though she claims to get rid of some things. She wears baggy shirts, and multi-coloured hand made leather shoes. She has drunk 1664 out of a can at the tender age of 75 at a hotel in Paris and with a big smile on her face would even be tempted to run a walking stick along public railings. She would be horrified at the thought of spitting in public or nicking the neighbours flowers – her own are far superior.

***

Returning to my host and newly found companion I consider what I can communicate in the sketch. Ben is very caring, considerate and supportive but cryptically encoded. There is a playful fun side that is well hidden behind the serious, intellectual and analytical veneer. With this in mind I pull out a 6B pencil, outline the face and start work on the eyes, which I have found are a bluish colour in certain light and an almost greyish/bluish colour in other light. Two hours later, two eyes are staring back at me. All the pencils have taken up occupancy on the desk and left their mark on both my fingers and the new putty rubber. Satisfied with the result I abandon my artistic endeavours for the evening.

***

After a supper of toast and avocado I raid Ben's music collection and discover that he has the typical student CDs of the 80s and 90s. I pick out Tracy Chapman and listen to it whilst snuggled into my sleeping bag on the sofa. A colleague once described Chapman's music as nice. I recall asking why some people insist on wearing their stupidity on their sleeve and getting into a great deal of bother. Fortunately, it was in my days of lesser tolerance. Now I like to remember the words of Confucius, 'Silence is a friend that does not betray.'

The words of the song, 'Talking Bout a Revolution,' are very powerful, 'Poor people gonna rise up and get their share, poor people gonna rise up and take what's theirs... And finally the tables are starting to turn, talkin' bout revolution.'

The lyrics force me to think about the poor of this country. Will they ever get their share or what is rightly theirs? At the end of the CD I lie in silence for a while. I then play Labi Siffre and after listening to the first song, 'Something inside so strong,' I retire for the night with some of the lyrics playing in my head.

'The higher you build your barriers
The taller I become
The farther you take my rights away
The faster I will run...'

There is always hope.

Sunday 6th November...

It's nearly lunchtime and I have drawn Ben's nose, mouth, cheeks and chin. All I need to do now are the teeth, ears, hair and neck. Physically it is looking like Ben and the resemblance is definitely there. However, I don't think I can fully capture the personality behind the image until I get to know him a bit better. That said the warm smile is certainly evident. My stiff neck and shoulders force me to leave the desk and go in search of lunch and a cake for Ben's birthday. Even at the other side of the world everyone needs a cake on his or her birthday. I bought the birthday card in England. Outside it is another glorious day with not a cloud in the sky. As usual I cream up with factor 35 and grab my shades.

The streets of Mariscal are devoid of cars and people. I ignore all the quiet restaurants and end up in one attached to a hostel. The place is full of Europeans drinking large beers and planning their trips. I see numerous copies of the Lonely Planet and piles of adventure brochures – mountain climbing, rafting, horse riding, and biking. I spot The Biking Dutchmen brochure and remember the down hill cycle ride that I did four years earlier. You drive to the top of a steep mountain and cycle down. I decorated my body with bruises of various sizes and designs by falling off three times and shook myself silly whilst dancing over the rocky terrain. After the third fall the guide tied some knee pads to my elbows as well – I didn't fall again! At the end of the cycle ride I asked to sit on the roof of the minibus to get a better view of the surrounding mountains. Not only did I get to enjoy the mountains I also experienced the branches of several trees up close and personal. I don't think that I will be repeating the experience on this occasion.

I ignore the backpackers and find a quiet table next to some locals. I notice that the food is local food with a choice of beef or fish. I can't do either choice. Given that for Sikhs the cow is sacred, beef is not an option. And fish just tends to come up for air rather violently. I ask for a plate of vegetables and get just that with some rice and beans. All it needs is a bit of spice and a chapatti. As I eat I continue to observe the life in the restaurant. My eyes follow the movements of a little girl probably no more than 6 years old. She is in a summer dress that she has out grown by two sizes and is wearing a pair of worn sandals. She moves from table to table begging money off the tourists but everyone shoos her away without even looking at her. She eventually makes her way over to my table. I invite her to sit down and offer her my untouched complementary fizzy drink. She sits opposite me and sips the drink through the straw without taking her big eyes off me. Her long black hair is uncombed but platted and her skin is a leathery dark brown colour. As she wraps both her hands around the glass I can see the dirt under her chewed finger nails and cuticles. She utters a few words that are incomprehensible and puts her hand out. I say I have no money so she sips a bit more and leaves. I finish my meal pay the bill and leave. Walking up the street I notice the little girl with her mother and brother. On the 6 de Deciembre I buy a piece of cake and candles. Once back at the house I crack on with the sketch and have it completed to a satisfactory standard by 7pm. Next I turn to the work that I need to prepare for the children.

***

It's nearly midnight when I am woken by the creaking front door. I stagger out of bed to wish Ben a happy birthday and bring out the cake. As he is telling me about his rugby tournament – which his team won – I give him his birthday cards – one from me and one from Dom and ask him to stay in the living room. I return two minutes later carrying the slice of chocolate cake decorated with a single lit candle – the small cake could not accommodate 40 candles. Ben blows out the candle, laughs and says, 'You're nuts.'

I thought Dom had passed on that crucial bit of information. He eats a mouthful and comments that it is good cake. I decline the offer to try some as I had already prepared my teeth for bed. We agree to celebrate properly with a meal out at the weekend. As it is late and Ben has his usual 6am start we bid each other goodnight.

Monday 7th November...

It's Monday afternoon and I really do need a cuppa to deal with the trauma of the day. Fuelled with Cornflakes, coffee and a banana I whizzed down to the taxi rank on Madrid. I got into the back of the taxi that was at the front of the queue, greeted the driver and told him my destination. I was somewhat surprised when he switched off the meter and quoted a fare of $5 dollars. I confidently said that I would not pay that amount and offered $2. I wanted to add that the concept of bartering is Indian and that I had it to a fine art. Incredulously he declined – clearly the skills needed to be fine tuned. I got out the taxi and went to the next one along. To my horror this chap even refused to take me there. 'Why?' I asked.

'Because I won't,' he replied.

Defeated but determined I walked over to the 12 de Octubre and flagged one down. But again I was refused. Standing on the corner of Mariscal and 12 de Octubre I was not only mourning the loss of my comfort mobile but also wondering how the hell I would get to work. Annoyed and fed up and everything else that goes with such a state but still determined I dragged myself kicking and screaming down to Agosto to catch the Trole. On the way it suddenly dawned on me that I caught a taxi with ease last week as it was a national holiday and there was virtually no traffic on the main roads. Normal chaos had resumed this morning with the usual incessant car horns and buses churning out insane quantities of black fumes. 15 minutes later I was sitting on the Trole having battled with a turnstile that did not want to turn. Three stops down and just as I relaxed and recomposed myself, I realised that I was going in the wrong direction. Is it a normal human reaction to feel embarrassed and to imagine that everyone knows that you are going the wrong way? I told myself off for my irrationality got off and caught the bus going the other way and paid another 25 centavos for the pleasure. I successfully arrived at the Place de Santa Domingo and walked up the side streets, past the sleeping drunks, to the project. It was impossible to miss the prostitutes promoting their goods alongside the other street vendors. This was too much to digest at 9.10am in the morning and I simply looked up at the Virgin Mary. I couldn't wait to find out what surprises the project had in store.

***

Iki and I were in the middle of the alphabet when the so-called social worker and teacher marched into the room and took all the children, except the disabled ones, into the other classroom. No explanation was offered and there was no please or thank you. The social worker had decided to teach them personal safety. Iki and I could hear the children chanting a poem – so no marks for originality. I sat in the room and watched for five minutes. The children had learnt the personal safety poem by heart and were chanting it subconsciously. The social worker was trying to focus their attention on the white board where she had neatly written the poem. I wanted to point out that they could not read so there was no point in them staring at the words, but I didn't bother. The children were bored and restless and wanted to leave the room. I was very bored and left. I used the opportunity to raid the office for resources. But all I found was another storybook and some old half-used colouring books. The children were abruptly returned to us but just in time for their story. They chose Sleeping Beauty and El Patio Feo. Jacson momentarily sat on my lap but was soon pushed aside by Julia. I compromised by moving so that they could sit on either side of me. Both attempted to grab my nit protector. I opted for a tight fitting baseball cap following Iki's advice – the head scarf just didn't carry the same street cred. As Julia lent forward I could see the nits in her hair. In fact all the children desperately needed a shower and a change of clothes. I told Iki that I could not stay and help as I had Spanish lessons in the afternoon.

The time with the second group went smoothly with no interruptions from either the social worker or the teacher. Even Julia only interrupted the one time and seemed satisfied when I said that I would see her in the morning. I gave my first Spanish test – having rehearsed the words over the weekend – and helped Heidi to progress with the alphabet. This morning she was allowed to attend the class for the duration. Teaching her was hard work as she was more interested in telling me that she wanted to live with me and wanted me to be her mum. I was lost for words as I looked at her pretty face. At 12 noon the teacher walked in and said, 'Vamos niños.'

I replied, 'En dos minutos,' – the Spanish was starting to come.

Swords had been drawn ready for battle and from the corner of my eye I could see Iki watching both myself and the teacher. There was a momentary stand off and the teacher responded, 'Ahora.'

Silence prevailed. It was a crucial point in the battle that needed to be won – to make the point that we here to help and not be treated badly, I replied, 'No, en dos minutos, gracious.'

With raised eyebrows the teacher left the room. Iki stared at me and burst out laughing and the children just smiled. Rather like Manuel in the comedy

Faulty Towers, 'Que,' was my only comment. Two minutes later we dismissed the children with a list of words that they had to learn for tomorrow's spelling test. Iki walked with me to the Trole as she was desperate for some fresh air. In the square we sat down on the concrete steps and shared my cheese sandwich. I listened to Iki's frustrations about the morning. 10 minutes later I left her where she was and jumped on the Trole back to Mariscal in time for my Spanish lesson.

The two hours of Spanish although demanding were more manageable and the time flew by. We covered the family topic. I learnt that the family is very important and the cornerstone of life in Ecuador. All activity centres on the family – I found this to be a totally alien concept. When Mercedes asked me to tell her about my family I smiled and said nothing for a few moments. I wanted to say that it is just a normal family – in that it's as typically dysfunctional as any other family of modern times. I wanted to add that the family is an interesting social construct that perhaps needs to be deconstructed and then reconstructed in some meaningful way. But instead I chose to respect Mercedes beliefs and described my family of mother, father, one sister and three brothers. This led to uninteresting conversation about the benefits of a large family. Mercedes was so impressed with my progress that she gave me three pieces of homework. Now at 6.00pm with the homework done and schoolwork prepared I relax with my cuppa. So very English! Ben is due back in half an hour and had threatened to bring Paul's scrabble set with him. So tonight the challenge could commence.

***

This epic game of scrabble certainly spread across the four corners of the board. It was a game of two halves. The first half of 2 hours was slightly longer than the second half of 1½ hours. The hour-long interval at 9.00pm at the local restaurant was needed to feed the fading bodies. I still can't believe that a two-letter word worth 64 points cost me this first game. I appreciate that when I'm mentally very tired my sentences can become incoherent, as my brain tends to jumble up the word order. I even acknowledge that after a day of speaking Spanish I end up saying things like coffee black or water without gas. But even I couldn't accept that QI was anything other than Ben empathising with my verbal dyslexia – or winding me up. Not surprisingly I challenged him when he placed the Q above the letter I in the word intent and then smugly put the I next to it above the letter N in the same word. At the start of the game we had agreed to use my imported pocket Oxford English dictionary, the pamphlet that accompanied the game which contained a list of two letter words, and the on-line scrabble dictionary to check any challenges. I was mortified when the computer confirmed that the word QI actually existed. We discovered that the QI is a variant spelling of the word Chi. The 22nd letter of the Greek alphabet led to my downfall. I did later throw in my own two letter words all of which Ben challenged unsuccessfully. My words included EA – river, EE (Scottish word for eye) and AI, which is not a variant spelling of the Yorkshire word aye. According to the scrabble dictionary Ai is a shaggy coated, slow moving animal of South America. Given the amount of time Ben took over each move, I was convinced that he had the characteristics of an Ai. Having drawn first blood by forty points Ben went to bed wearing a Cheshire cat smile. I calculated that the loss was greater but Ben pointed out that I had added my own score up incorrectly – perhaps I have numerical dyslexia too.

Tuesday 8th November…

It's 5pm and I finish my cuppa before diving into my homework and school work for the children. Today was a good day and we were able to stick to and deliver the lesson plans. Knowing our luck this is likely to be the calm before the storm. The first group for some reason decided that I should draw them Mickey Mouse as two of the boys were wearing donated t-shirts with cartoon transfers of Mickey. I took the black marker and sketched Mickey on the white board. The two boys stood nearby with their small chests stuck out so that I could see the image. It was really hard not to burst out laughing. Iki made up for this and creased up laughing at the sight as she walked into the classroom. The kids liked it so much that I agreed to do some outline sketches on A4 paper for them to colour them in. I am drawing the seventh Mickey on paper donated by Muriel when Ben walks in. He looks at the drawings, shakes his head, wanders off into his chill out room and jumps into the hammock. He's still recovering from his rugby tournament and just like yesterday will be out cold for the next half hour.

***

It's 10.00pm and I have just lost the second game of scrabble. Ben has won by 10 points. How outrageous is that? Ben has been suckered into a false sense of security and now it's time for a comeback. I jokingly tell Ben that he is winning because he is taking so long to have his turn. I remind him that tonight's game has taken 2 hours and 40 minutes. I suggest playing for a fixed period of time and Ben proposes a chess clock. Within minutes he is on the case and twenty minutes later has a chess clock downloaded onto his computer. We discover that this only offers five minutes each way but just for a laugh I suggest playing a ten minute game of scrabble. Ben tells me I'm mad but concedes to the madness. And mad and furious it is indeed with hands racing to grab handfuls of tiles, throw words onto the board, scribble down the scores and switch the chess clock. There is no time for dilly dallying and barely enough time to add up the scores let alone throw in challenges. But Ben is well beat and I hit a score of 250. He demands a rematch but loses again. In this third game we lose track of scores, the time has expired and we both surrender in fits of laughter. Ben tells me that playing for 10 minutes is mad and a more suitable clock is needed. He is back on the computer at which point I excuse myself and head for bed.

Wednesday 9th November...

Yesterday was definitely the calm before today's storm. I am in desperate need of some personal space and solitude and head straight home after Spanish. The racket of music emanating from the house reminds me that it is Gladys day. She is glad to see me and launches into 100 miles an hour

Spanish. When she pauses for breath I quickly jump in and ask her to speak a little slower. She laughs and grabs my checks, which is something that I have not experienced since I was about 10 years old – even back then I had concluded that it was very strange adult behaviour. I expected her to add the phrase, 'Chubby cheeks,' and offer me a sweet. Instead I offer to make her a cup of tea which she accepts. Whilst the kettle is boiling I learn a bit more about Gladys. She is married with grown up children and several grandchildren. I discovered after my first week that Gladys likes to play hide and seek – she hides things and we spend all week looking for them just to have her hide them again. The other day I was looking for the sugar. It is in a plastic container with a bright red lid and typically stored in the cupboard. But alas it had been moved to some other location. Ben and I checked every cupboard in the kitchen and the pantry but there was no sign of the sugar. Just as we had given in, Ben looked in the fridge. Hey presto, the sugar was sat comfortably next to the milk – of course. Today the sugar is still in the cupboard. Gladys helpfully washes, irons and puts all our clothes on our respective beds. However, each week we find ourselves returning items of clothing to each other – at least there is no mistaking the bras, well at least I hope not! With my limited Spanish, I tell Gladys that I am working with street children in the old town and learning Spanish. I have reached the stage in Spanish where I can talk about myself on a basic level and be understood. The next stage is to understand what anyone else might be saying to me and replying appropriately. As Gladys has a rural accent and holds the world record for speed talking this adds to my challenge.

***

I take my cup of tea and head for the hammock. Actually, I want to head towards my fish pond. The post-it note on the computer, 'Downloading chess clock, do not turn off,' forces a smile on a bad day. I drink my tea, put on my shades and close my eyes. A few deep breaths later I find myself sitting on the beach at Abel Tasmin. Maybe my journey really did begin here. All is calm and I can feel a gentle breeze blowing across my face. As I look out to the distant horizon, I reflect without interruption. The membership of the first group had changed. Three of the children aged 5 to 6 had returned home but were replaced by three new children that the teacher dumped in the classroom at 9.00am. As usual, no information was provided. One child could not communicate. He spoke but we could not understand. The second child, who was crying when he entered the class, refused to speak and ran out. The third was a 9 year old pressure cooker at the point of explosion. I asked him to sit well away from Michael and Jacson. Within two minutes the teacher frog marched the crying boy back into the room and forced him to sit down. The more she forced him the more he refused. Disturbed by the scene, I asked Iki what was going on. She explained that the teacher wanted the boy in the class but that he wanted to be with his brother who was in carpentry. I stepped in and suggested that the child be allowed to leave the room and be with his brother.

Just as I finished speaking the pressure cooker exploded and threw a wooden table across the room just missing one of the younger children. The situation was about to spiral out of control. I could see that the stress was starting to take its toll on double-trouble who were becoming more and more agitated and throwing things on the floor. It was time to take control. I asked Iki to take the crying child to his brother and ordered the pressure cooker out of the room. The teacher said that he had to stay because it was important for him to learn. I looked at the teacher and said that she could teach him today as I was not having him in the room with the other children. There was no room for negotiation. The teacher took the child out of the class.

I turned to the remaining children, Michael, Jacson, Julia, Jairo, Antonia, Henry, Naila and the new child and said good morning. Iki returned and I proposed letting them all just do a range of activities, colouring, story telling, playing and to have a long play break. Everyone just needed to chill out. The rest of the session went well. During the break I had all the children playing football with a new football that we found hoarded in one of the cupboards in the social workers office. Mickey Mouse was well received and the children spent 20 minutes colouring in their individual drawings. I observed that Jacson was totally absorbed in this practical activity. We helped the children to tape the finished work to the wall. The white background was certainly beginning to vanish.

Just when you think things can't get worse they always do. At 10.35am Iki and I began to wonder what had happened to the second group. They are always prompt. I suggested that we both go up and find out. We were told that the older children had to continue with the carpentry at the request of Scary Nun. When I asked about the whereabouts of the nuns I was told that that they were in prayers. On hearing this I told the kids to change out of their overalls and follow me. Michael the volunteer offered me a supportive smile and then pulled a straight face. Even in the midst of crisis my mind has its own sense of humour. I pictured Ganesha and imagined him taking a child in each of his hands and escorting them downstairs. Ganesha is the Hindu elephant headed deity, with four hands and a huge pot-bellied body of a human being. His transport is a mouse. I imagined the reaction of the nuns to the sight of Ganesha and wondered whether the mouse would send them screaming. On the way I saw Heidi and José in the kitchen and collected them as well. The cook tried to protest by saying that she needed Heidi. I simply replied, 'Despues,' and added, 'Thank you,' as I walked away. I knew that given her very generous proportions she was hardly likely to chase after me. In the class I looked at Iki and said, 'Let's teach.' No one entered the class and at 12 noon we told the kids that we would see them in the morning and gave them their homework.

The bad day was over or so I thought. However, straight after came the bad icing on the bad cake of a day. As I walked over to the Trole I noticed that it was unusually quiet, so quiet that there was no one waiting to catch a bus. As I approached the ramp I saw a white sheet of paper flapping against the glass doors. It simply read, 'No servicio.' I hadn't planned for this eventuality. I tried to flag down a cab but to no avail. The cabs either had passengers and those that didn't simply refused to go to Mariscal. No Trole, no taxi, and no map – life without a map. What a pickle. I looked up at the skies and uttered, 'Now what?' and the solution to my problem stared right back at me. Of course the overhead cables that power the Trole were the map back to Mariscal – perhaps there is always a map. On Agosto I walked into a public protest. Protestors were protesting and police were lined up behind riot shields in front of a building. Given the sheer number of police officers, I assumed this to be a government building. Although there was a great deal of shouting, chanting and waving of banners the protest seemed peaceful. People not involved in the protest went about their daily business. The road was closed to vehicles which explained the cancelled Trole service and why I could not get a taxi.

Before going to my Spanish class, I visited Ecuador Volunteers, met with the director and discussed what happened. We talked about the project and the role of volunteers. He explained in depth the history of difficulties that his organisation had experienced with the project. Some of what he disclosed was very worrying and included the mistreatment of children. He added that he was in the process of collating information for a report with which he could take action. At the end of the meeting we agreed that he would contact the senior nun, mother superior, and facilitate the delivery of our programme. I discovered that Scary Nun is not the senior nun. If she was it would elevate her status to that of Super Scary Nun, which was a very scary thought indeed. As I left I paid Maria my outstanding volunteer fee of $60 and handed in the receipt for $20 for the story books that I bought. The money had been next to my sweaty feet all morning – I figured that no one would steal my trainers and therefore the money would be safe. Now I am trying to work out what bits of my behaviour were acceptable and what bits weren't. I really must get the teacher on side and get her to work with us so that the work can continue once we leave. But what can I do with the nuns and the issues raised by the director. Ben's voice brings me back and I have totally lost my train of thoughts.

***

It's time to vacate the hammock and sort out the work for tomorrow. Ben wastes no time in taking up the vacant seat. 'It's nice and warm,' I tell him. In his hand I notice my little green booklet, 'How to solve cryptic crossword puzzles.' He has taken ownership and is ploughing through it. I suspect that we will be doing the daily Guardian crosswords next. I leave him to it. Sitting at the dining room table I realise that I have learnt all the regular and common irregular verbs in the present tenses, the simple future tense and I am now in the process of learning the past tenses which is the focus of tonight's homework. Once I have tackled these I will select a list of words for the second group and draw more cartoon characters for the first group. Perhaps I will introduce Pluto and Goofy.

Thursday 10th November...

It's Thursday evening and we are testing out the electronic chess clock. Last night we were both too tired to engage the brains in any intellectual activity. We have set each clock for 20 minutes and agreed that anyone who runs out of time will forfeit 10 points for each additional minute taken thereafter until the end of the game. The game has already gone on for an hour because Ben keeps pausing to challenge my two letter words. Over a third of the board is completely blocked and it's hard work getting rid of the remaining letters. I have just played out and left Ben holding the letter Q; there was no spare letter I to play off. My winning stroke was probably the letter X on the triple letter score between two Is. So I beat him with the 14th letter of the Greek alphabet. That's sweet. The joint score is just under 500 and there are no exciting or wacky words. After a brief post mortem Ben suggests a rematch. I concede and ask him to set up while I change the music. It's time for a bit of UB40. It's 50 minutes later I have just beaten him again. Ben thought he had got off to a cracking start by playing a seven letter word, 'Dispute.' His smile was soon banished as I played the word, 'Bemused.' It was one not to be disputed! This has been a good game and overall the joint score is respectably near 600 points. I have secured victory by 25 points. Ben is going through the scores. Two minutes later tells me that I have added my score up incorrectly and in his favour. I have actually beaten him by 33 points. He adds that maths is not my strong point. I dare not tell him that I did pure and applied maths to A level. The score is 2 games each and tonight I'm wearing the Cheshire cat smile. It's mine all mine and I'm taking it to bed.

Before bidding each other goodnight we agree to celebrate Ben's birthday at the local Italian restaurant tomorrow night.

***

Lying in bed I suddenly remember to set my alarm an hour earlier than usual – being allergic to mornings the early start will be a shock to the system. Tomorrow is my first day as a volunteer at Ben's school. I will be a classroom assistant in one of the junior classes and help as needed until the end of term. My attire will be smart casual and I will even wear my watch. In one week I will go from working with the poorest in this society to working with the richest. Thinking about the poorest, this morning went very, very smoothly and was enjoyable. I was a little surprised to be allowed back into the building after yesterday's events. I physically bumped into Scary Nun who simply raised her eyebrows as she walked past. People seem to keep on doing this in my presence. The core composition of the first group hadn't changed and we even allowed the pressure cooker back into the classroom on the understanding that we could ask him to leave if he started to steam. Incredibly he was well behaved and reluctantly did some work. We let the crying child remain with his brother – a decision that the teacher did not contest. I will never forget the most amazing moment of the day – out of the blue, Julia uttered, 'A, e, i, o, u,' with complete clarity.

The world of the classroom came to a complete standstill as all the children stared at Julia in utter bewilderment. It was indeed a magical moment. The look of shock on Jacson's face was a sight to behold. He opened his mouth but was not sure what to say so closed it again. Even the pressure cooker, who had tried to bully her, conceded a smile. Momentarily, Iki and I were equally dumbstruck but then became jubilant and gave Julia a big hug. She responded with her usual cheeky grin and carried on scribbling. She had settled down and craved less attention. She seemed to know that we cared. How I wish I could access her inner world and help her.

The second group were the usual delight and eager to learn. They asked for a 15 word spelling test rather than 10. I am building words around themes;

weather, fruits, family, vegetables, animals, household items, etc. Most of these children can tackle long addition but struggle with subtraction especially with the concept of carrying one over. They are certainly making progress and demand homework every lunchtime. The words, 'Mi tarea,' get chanted five minutes before the end of the class. Half way through the lesson we heard a noise from the other class and stopped in our tracks. As we had just finished the spelling test I suggested a five minute break. Whilst Iki went to investigate I introduced noughts and crosses. Soon the whole board was covered with noughts and crosses in colours of red, black and blue. The children clearly enjoyed themselves and it gave me an idea for future lessons. Perhaps we can have a short break every lesson. I could introduce them to dot to dot which in Spanish would be, 'Punto a punto.' Iki returned with a huge smile across her face and told me that the teacher was sat reading to the members of the first group. Miracles do happen I told myself.

Saturday 12th November...

It's Saturday morning and I am sitting in the garden next to my imaginary fish pond but it's not the same as the real thing. I wonder how the fish are doing. It is coming into winter so they will be fairly dormant. I remember the time when during their first winter I didn't see any of them for nearly four weeks and thought that they had perished – but they put me out of my misery and came to the surface on a winter's day when the sun was shining. Here, today, the sun is shining in a cloudless sky. Ben is sat at the computer reading the minute by minute football commentary of the Palace match. I close my eyes and drift off. As Ben and Paul jointly own the car, Ben usually collects him on the way to school. Yesterday Ben made an additional stop on a street corner to pick up the temporary biology teacher called Tamara. After brief introductions we all exchanged pleasantries. Tamara told me that she spent her teenage years at an international school in Quito but is of Dutch heritage. She is now back here on a temporary basis to decide what to do with her life – as you do! The drive to the school was sensational and one that you could not tire of – the valley with its meandering river and the surrounding mountains were uplifting. I wanted Ben to keep driving through the glorious hills and valleys until the sun went down. Sadly, after about 40 minutes we arrived at the school which is located in the valley. Not surprisingly, it is behind locked metal gates that are staffed by guards. Ben introduced me to the year 3 class teacher and then left me to it. He had arranged for my lunches to be charged to his card. As this was my first visit to the school, whilst waiting for the children to arrive, I took in the surroundings. I was very impressed with all the bright flowers and blossom – the reds, oranges and purples provided a happiness of colour. It reminded me of some of the flowers and blossom that I had seen around Quito. The heavily pregnant avocado trees were ready to come forth in abundance – a magnificent sight. It was very tempting to pick some fruit but I refrained. I pictured myself swimming in the odd shaped pool and beholding the surrounding mountains. When I was introduced to the children the first thing that struck me was that they were all pale skinned and clearly of European heritage. In fact a majority of the children in the school were of a similar background. I suddenly felt like a minority. My early morning tasks were to mark various bits of homework and help with the maths test – Ben would have laughed if he knew. Mid morning I helped another class with the IT session. Caz's daughter Jesse was in this class – I had forgotten that she attended the school. She recognised me straight away and waved. Later on I heard her say, 'Es mi amiga,' to her friends.

After a most enjoyable lunch I listened to the children read and attended the assembly. It was an easy day as the whole syllabus is conducted in English and children are not allowed to speak any Spanish in the classroom. At the end of the day I sat and watched some children being driven away in expensive chauffeur driven cars whilst others were taken home in the school buses.

I can't help but compare these children with those at the project. These children have everything, health, wealth and happiness and a secure future. Most importantly these children are able to live and enjoy their childhood without a care in the world. I am happy for these children but weep for the ones that have nothing and have already lived a lifetime of experience that is written across their prematurely aged hands and faces. Children at the project can only dream of having a different life, to one day realise that they are not ugly ducklings but beautiful swans. Their dreams are lived out in fairly tales – the dreams of the children at the school are lived out in reality. One of the teachers told me that some of the five year olds are still dressed by their maids. I wanted to tell her about the little five-year old that washes her own clothes in cold water. The lottery of life! Ben shouts out the score from the living room. I decide to make myself a cup of tea.

***

I take out an armchair and put it in the garden out of the direct sun. Drinking my tea I think about last night. The food at the Italian restaurant was excellent. I must e-mail Dom and thank him as he had sent me a cheque for £50 to treat Ben to a birthday meal. Ben and I worked out that we could do two meals for that amount of money and agreed to extend his birthday celebrations over a few weeks. I offered to treat him to a Greek at the restaurant opposite the Italian. Over dinner I learnt that Ben does not drink much – just the occasional beer or gin and tonic after a hard day at work. No smoking, no caffeine and almost no alcohol. I didn't tell him that Dom and I cemented our friendship one Friday evening over a bottle of gin – previous to that we didn't like each other very much. I foolishly agreed to a drinking competition – the first under the table. Not the thing to do as a novice with an experienced drinker. Our friends returned to the house to find us both sitting on the floor. We were quite happily chatting away. I never did drink gin again after that night. The following day, I discovered hangovers and Dom not surprisingly was fine and dandy. Ben talked about his plans to retire from teaching in 12 years time and had done the maths. I just smiled and shook my head. He asked about my plans. What could I say other than I was a recovering workaholic who had decided to take a drastic step to restore the work/life balance by having no work plan for the foreseeable future. We spent a bit more time getting to know each other. We calculated that we last met at Dom's wedding 10 years earlier and only a couple of times before then. I updated Ben on the roller coaster happenings at the project and invited him to visit which he was keen to do. I said I would try and arrange a visit for a weekend day. I warned Ben that it would be very different from the school but at least he wouldn't require a nit hat. We talked about the condemned cooker and decided that the priority for the weekend was to buy a new one. We would fit this in-between going to the school bonfire night, a brunch on Sunday with some of the rugby crowd and the weekly shop at Mega Maxi.

***

I finish my tea and get on with some gardening. Actually I'm dispatching the lilies to an early grave as they are choking me. Whilst getting rid of the lilies I find some flowers that have dried beautifully in the sun and decide to pick them. Gardening is also my excuse for delaying doing my homework and the work for my children. I am pleased as I have managed to get free resources and the children now have their own exercise books; A5 for the younger ones and A4 for the older ones. However, I cannot disclose my wonderful source. I take the dried flowers indoors and Ben momentarily shifts his eyes from the computer screen. I explain that they are dried flowers that I intend to sketch at some stage. I sit down at the dining room table and open my text book. I seem to have taken permanent ownership of the table and it is always cluttered with my work. Ben on the other hand is extremely tidy. I apologise for the mess and promise to clean up. Ben addresses the bomb site, calls me a girlie swot and continues reading his commentary. After the football match we pop out to the local shops to price up cookers. I'm shocked to find that the price of the cheapest cooker is equivalent to the average monthly salary. Ben is particular and wants one with a grill – to do important things like cheese on toast or as he puts it, 'To grill a juicy steak.' It's his sense of humour knowing that I do not eat beef. He draws up a short-list but I suspect that he has already chosen the one that he wants. We discuss the possibilities over a late lunch at a local Chinese restaurant, before heading off to support the school bonfire night.

***

If you run a British school abroad, I guess that you do all things British including the celebration of Guy Fawkes Night. This event is well organised and well supported by the parents. The evening kicks off as young people from the upper school deliver a well rehearsed play – I am impressed by their talent and self-confidence. As the sun goes down the temperature drops drastically but no one is cold as there is a huge fire in the middle of the tarmac football pitch – it is burning like a furnace. All we need are football sized marsh mellows and very long stakes. Sitting near the fire, I use the opportunity to talk to the teachers, parents and some children in my class. Periodically, Ben finds me and asks if I am alright – so considerate. At the end of the evening the fund-raising done by the children has raised nearly $90 for charity. I offer my project as a worthy cause and explain the ways in which I could use the money. I'm offered the funds and accept without hesitation. What a result – so all the networking skills developed as a suit are put to good use.

On the way home I share my ideas for spending the money. I definitely want to spend it on the children and not on resources for the project – I've been told that resources tend to vanish. I tell Ben that I want to buy each child that I work with a toothbrush and a tube of toothpaste, their own set of colouring pencils, as well as a pen, pencil, rubber and sketch pad. I also want to buy a unique gift for each child – something that they will like. Jacson is mad about aeroplanes, Michael likes marbles and Jairo is obsessed by toy cars. The older group of girls will like doing craft activities. I explain that I know it's not much but at least they will have things that they can call their own. Ben points out that I only have $90. I smile and say that I have pledges from friends back at home.

Sunday 12th November...

It's Sunday morning and I am lazing in bed with a coffee and a cryptic crossword. Our games of scrabble are interspersed with crossword puzzles and internet countdown. Ben has made good use of my cryptic crossword book and is more than half way through. He has promised me a synopsis – he will hold onto the book to help reduce the excess luggage on my return journey! I have handed my 350 Telegraph cryptic crossword book of puzzles to Caz who is a total addict. This leaves me with the book of The Sun crossword puzzles. It's 10.30 and time to check the destruction that Ben is causing in the kitchen – he is certainly making a lot of noise. He muttered something about making some humus and guacamole to take to the brunch. He made both dips for the recent trip to Mindo and I have to admit they were very good – it's a family recipe that cannot be disclosed – and therefore I am excused from offering to help. For the sake of my allergy he makes the humus without lemon juice. I walk into the kitchen to find that just like his brother Ben has managed to use every pot and pan. I sneak a taste – this batch is equally as good – but get caught in the act. Ben jokingly waves a lemon over the dips. I pull my sad face and take another mouthful before making my escape to the bathless bathroom. I am looking forward to lunch as it will give me the opportunity to practice my Spanish with Ximena.

***

Ximena is impressed with the progress that I have made over the past few weeks. She adds that I have gained a good command of the grammar and speak better than Ben. I ask her not to tell Ben – he already calls me a, 'Girlie swot.' As I speak she kindly corrects the errors for which I thank her. We revert to French when I do not know the word or phrase in Spanish. I really like this woman and I know that she will make a great mother. From the short time I have known her I have observed how she has lovingly spoken to her unborn child and gently stroked her stomach as if stroking the head of her daughter. She talks about the forthcoming wedding. She is hoping that the wedding can go ahead by mid December – I gather that marrying a foreigner in this country is a complicated business. After a splendid brunch and good champagne Ben and I head off to look at more cookers – Ben is determined to buy one in the forthcoming week.

Tuesday 15th November...

I am walking home having just offered my apologies for tomorrow's Spanish class. Sometimes life presents you with choices – Spanish lessons or thermal baths and champagne. This was the choice that Ben offered me at the pub quiz last night. After much deliberation – well at least five seconds I chose the obvious. Sadly we were being the English abroad. You find an English pub with an English name, Reina Victoria or Queen Victoria, serving English beer and watch English football. On this occasion it was the pub quiz rather than the football. In the pub we found a big group of English tourists. They were all from Manchester, spoke with broad Manchurian accents and were seasoned quiz contestants. Ben, Tamara and I huddled around a small round table and named ourselves the, 'Scrabble bugs,' which was probably the extent of my contribution to the proceedings. The categories included films, you are here, music, TV soaps, sports and anything goes. In the film section we managed to get one right – South American films or film directors was evidently not our speciality. We made up for our short-fall on the music section where we wisely played our joker. Ben did rather well at the quick fire rounds between the categories and won two shooters – you had to be the first to name the country of origin of obscure beers. As a non-drinker Ben knew them all. He is right when he says that his head is full of useless information. I half suspect that it is all logically filed. We took third place and won a pitcher of beer. This we distributed to the neighbouring tables as Tamara didn't drink beer, I discovered a nice wine and Ben was driving.

***

Although Mercedes accepted my apologies she still gave me homework in preparation for Thursday's lessons. Like a good student I am going to get this done before Ben returns from school. Standing in the kitchen I admire the new cooker that arrived yesterday. It has a grill and my rumbling tummy reminds me that I have not had anything to eat since breakfast. I put the grill to good use and make myself cheese on toast with Marmite. It's simply yummy. I digest it with a cup of Yorkshire tea whilst reading about the trip in Ben's guide – from the corner of my eye I can see the homework on my right but pretend it's not there. The thermal baths are in a village called Papallacta located about 70km east of Quito and at an altitude of 3,700m. Papallacta is a small settlement that has not been developed for tourism. The main attractions are the hot thermal baths and the various rambles. On a good day it is possible to see the snow-capped Antisana Mountain that stands proud at an altitude of 5,700m. Ben said that the place is a frequent haunt of teachers at the school and an overnight trip had been planned for tomorrow night. The group will be staying in wooden cabins owned by Hotel Termas de Papallacta. Everyone will be going straight from school and I will need to get there by 3.15pm. Ben had already drawn me a map – a right angle and a little square that represented the El Nacional training ground and had written the address of the school. There was no A3 map on this occasion. In response to my quizzical look, he expanded the map a little – he added a roundabout and the set of traffic lights where I would need to turn right. He suggested that I jump in a cab and ask the driver to go in the direction of Cumbaya and Tumbaco – the school was in the direction of Cununyacu. He offered to take my overnight bag in the car.

Wednesday 16th November...

Sitting in the taxi on my way to Ben's school I am saddened by this morning's news. I arrived at the project to find that Julia had left. The crying child and his brother had also returned home but their departure had less of an impact on me. We were not informed of Julia's imminent departure and we did not get the chance to say goodbye. Michael told us that she had been sent to an institution that supports disabled children and she was moved after Iki and I finished work yesterday. I'm sad and if I'm honest quite angry. I'm angry because no child is ever welcomed and no child ever has the chance to say goodbye. They come and they go but their journey is not marked in any way. It feels as if their lives simply do not matter.

***

'Donde ahora señora?'

The taxi driver has arrived at the El Nacional training ground and wants to know where to go. I look at Ben's map and ask the driver to turn right and drive a further 3km. I will add this to my memorabilia box and show it to Ben in 10 years time. I give my name, Ben's full name and speak to the receptionist in English before being allowed into the high-gated school.

Ben's first words are, 'Bad day?'

After a second I reply, 'Sad day, but never mind.'

It is a cloudy and wet journey but the thought of getting away feels good. When we arrive at Papallacta one of the teachers called Woody proposes going for a run and invites people to join him. Enthusiastically, I say it's a super idea and quickly change into my running gear – perhaps I can burn off my anger. It is my first run since the Great North Run and Ben tells me I'm nuts – again. After about five minutes my running partner is about 10 metres ahead of me, which is a small mercy. If I saw anyone in my state I would be dialling 999 and desperately trying to remember first aid skills that had not been used since finishing a four day training course. Physical fitness is not the problem – I have merely forgotten to take into account an altitude of 3,700m and my body is objecting. However, I let stupidity reign supreme and continue running. 20 minutes later I escape to the bathroom where I take some deep breaths. Perhaps I should have packed my inhalers.

'You're coughing,' is Ben's first comment as I join the rest of the group in the baths.

'It's nothing,' I tell him. I'm too embarrassed to say that I have forgotten my inhalers.

Over a glass or two of champagne I get to know the teachers a little better. I learn that some have been teaching at the school for a number of years, some are new and others are students on placement from America. Suitably relaxed and wrinkled from the hot water we dress for dinner and dine in the hotel restaurant. It is an agreeable meal. Walking back to the cabins after dinner we all stand in awe of Antisana, the snow capped top is contrasting beautifully with the blue of the night sky. There are no clouds and the stars are dancing in all their glory. Ansell Adams would have painstakingly captured this beautiful image on film. As it is quite late everyone goes to bed.

***

After an hour I am concerned that my coughing will wake the other people sleeping on the mezzanine floor so I quietly sneak out of bed. Ben is fast asleep in the next bed along. I step outside to a view that is even more breathtaking than before – to behold is to believe. I find a quiet spot and lie on my back. My thoughts return to my children at the project. Sadly some are imprisoned within the walls of the project until they are reclaimed by their families or moved to other institutions. They never go out unless taken on day trips organised by volunteers. This could explain why a few try to escape and risk life and limb whilst doing so. Is the fate of these children any different from the women prisoners that I met a few weeks earlier? What is their crime, other than being born into poverty and deprivation? Will life ever afford them the opportunity to absorb the beauty of such a night, to star gaze, to camp under the constellations? I have no answers but with each cold breath my anger leaves my body. To stop myself from freezing to death I return to the cabin and creep back into my bed.

Thursday 17th November...

It's 5.30am and Clare, Woody and I are making the most of an early morning soak before setting off. Everyone will be leaving at 6.30am to get back in time for the start of the school day. It is a cloudless and rainless morning and Clare is telling me that the drive back will be spectacular. Only half listening to her, I suddenly realise that I am shattered and wonder how on earth I will cope with the day ahead. As we are driving back we are indeed rewarded with some spectacular scenery and my only regret is not having the camera. Ben offers to drop me off at El Nacional Training ground where I can catch a bus to the Rio Coco bus terminal in Quito. He details the time that it will take and points out all the key landmarks that the bus will pass –

including the round about with the monument of a man on a bike. At Rio Coco I need to catch the Ecovia to Mariscal. I nod and quietly say, 'Coffee.'

***

I arrive at the project 20 minutes late and offer my apologies to Iki. I quickly explain why and she is keen to know more about the trip. Looking at the children I notice that the other half of Jacson is absent and ask where he is. Iki tells me that he too has gone. An uncle took him yesterday evening. I turn to Jacson who is refusing to settle and work. Iki explains that he has been like that since she arrived. Suddenly he takes off and two minutes later he is climbing the partition wall from the other side of the large classroom and throwing things about. I know that he is dealing with his loss in the only way he knows how. He has just lost his companion and no one has given him the time to express how he feels. The child he plays football with, the child he gets into mischief with, the child he protects, the child that he fights with and the child that is his only friend has gone. I am angry with myself as I do not have the language to help him come to terms with his loss. Most of my time is taken up dealing with Jacson. The magnitude of his loss hits me when he even refuses to sit in on story time. He is always the first to demand a story and always chooses El Patito Feo. Had his hope of a fairy tale ending also gone?

When the second group arrives I notice that Heidi is missing again. I am about to go and fetch her when one of the girls tells us that she left yesterday with an aunt. The girl whose name I could never remember had also returned home with her sister. Momentarily, I look at Heidi's exercise book and her name that she had written so proudly. The entire alphabet had been neatly copied. However, I have no time to mourn the losses as my attention is taken up by the new girl called Anna Gabriella. She is a 10 year old of African heritage and turned up in the night. I find that she is extremely bright and has had some good schooling. She reads and writes better than any other child in the room. All I am told is that she is at the project due to a family crisis.

Today we are teaching more geography. Two weeks ago this group did not know that they live in a city, which is part of a country and that there are many countries in the world. Before I joined the project, Iki had bought a world map and drawn outline sketches of South America for the children to colour. Holding up the map, Iki asks what happens when you reach the edge.

One child replies, 'You fall off.'

And another proposes that, 'You get lost.'

Following fits of laughter, Iki is trying to explain that the earth is round. I have an idea and shoot downstairs into the courtyard and return with the burst football – the new one had vanished and was probably reclaimed by the social worker. I re-inflate it as best as I can and say it is the earth. I stick a marker pen in the hole and rotate the ball while Iki explains that the earth rotates around its axis. The five children are totally absorbed as we show the movement of the earth in relation to the sun and the moon. Iki pretends that one of her rounded fists is the sun and the other the moon. They learn about day and night. I draw a sketch of the earth, moon and sun on the white board and the children eagerly copy it into their exercise books. After the daily spelling test, maths exercise and reading time we revise what they have learnt about the earth. Amazingly, they remember it all and explain what they have learnt in an animated way. The teacher interrupts to tell us it's lunchtime. I'm gob smacked as two of the children turn round and say, 'En cinco minutos, por favor.'

The teacher does not object and leaves us to it. As the children are about to leave, they demand their word list. I agree to write it out and bring it to the dining room. As Iki puts the tables and chairs away I write out a list of words five times. We agree that it has been a good morning although sad as we had lost so many children. She briefly talks about her plans for her birthday and invites Ben and me to join her and her boyfriend at a Mongolian restaurant on Monday. I accept the offer. Once we have cleared up she walks with me to the square. On the way she reminds me that it is her final week next week. Although I have already persuaded Michael to join me in the mornings I am saddened at the thought of Iki leaving. We have shared both the joy and the pain of the work and I respect her commitment and perseverance.

***

Having arrived just in time for my class – I walked back to Mariscal due to the weekly protest – my tutor wants to cancel my session and reschedule for Monday. I concede when she pleads that it suits her financially to have a student who wants to do four hour sessions and a new student wants to start today. For my willingness she produces some work sheets for next week. I walk off and find myself sitting in a local church, a very old church that is listed on the tourist map. There are no tourists. In fact I am alone. I don't know why I have chosen to sit in a church but welcome the silence and solitude that it offers. I am thinking about the children that have left the project and their future lives. I fear for Julia and Michael when I consider all the disabled beggars around the city. I am pleased that Heidi has escaped the slave labour of the kitchen and I hope that her aunt gives her the mothering that she so desperately craves. Before departing, I mentally leave all the children at the alter.

***

As my brain is craving caffeine and my stomach food I go in search of a restaurant. I stop at a place called La Torre Eifel in my own neighbourhood. Outside is a metallic replica of La Tour Eifel and curiosity leads me inside. As I enter the foyer I see that no one is about. I walk into the restaurant to find the noise from the television competing with that from the radio. All around are large images of everything Parisian. I am about to walk out again when a little man with dark curly hair and a moustache runs up to me and tells me that he is open. Absolutely starved by this stage I sit down. He asks if I would like the television or radio. I say neither. Obligingly, he runs to turn both off and returns with a menu. He asks what I would like to drink. I decide to abuse my body with that fizzy drink that I care not to promote. I need something substantial and order the chicken fajitas.

The food is freshly cooked and nicely spicy. As I eat, the owner hovers in and out of the room anxiously. I am so intrigued by his behaviour that I stop eating and give him my undivided attention. If he wrings his hands any more they are likely to twist off into a spin of their own. He hovers over and asks if the food is good. I tell him that it is excellent and give him a reassuring smile. I've concluded that he wants to ask me something but seems to be struggling with his words. Eventually he asks if I speak English. My affirmative answer forces a smile on his face but the wringing of the hands increases. I am about to conclude that he is a total head case when he asks if I would be willing to teach him English. I shock myself by agreeing to teach him on a weekly basis for a fee of $10 dollars an hour. He introduces himself as Santiago, the proprietor of La Torre Eifel. I give him my name and arrange the first lesson for Monday afternoon.

***

Completely replete, I pay and walk out into the street. It has just started to rain but the dark skies and the distant thunder suggest that it is likely to be another monsoon session and I beat a hasty retreat towards home. However, within seconds the heavy thunderous rain strikes and everyone is diving for cover. Typically the taxis have done a vanishing act and by the time I find shelter in a small café in the world trade centre I am soaked. I treat myself to a coffee and watch lots of wet suits take up occupancy around me. I talk to a young person who has sat down at my table. I learn that she has just graduated and has started work in an office as a trainee manager – I wonder if in 10 years time she will retain her enthusiasm. Every few minutes her mobile phone buzzes and she texts whilst talking to me. I am impressed by the speed with which her fingers move across the little device. Watching this behaviour I wonder if mobile mania is the same the world over. Over recent years I've watched people walk into lampposts, shop doors, other people as well as the paths of on coming cars. The offending object or person is always greeted with verbal abuse. I do find it increasingly difficult to distinguish between those that walk around talking to themselves and those that are talking to the device that seems surgically attached to their heads. I still can't concede to the concept of always being or needing to be contactable – even Muriel gave into the concept of texting before I did. Subconsciously, I frequently left my work mobile on planes, trains and offices all over the UK. Unfortunately, like a boomerang, it always came back – sometimes it returned to the office before I did and my secretary would comment, 'Your phone is on your desk, topped up, charged and ready to go.'

I remember the time when, in the middle of a senior meeting, I grabbed a colleague's star trek style phone, casually flicked it open and whispered the words, 'Beam me up.' His laughter brought the meeting to a halt and a severe scorn from the chair whilst I kept a straight face – I had to buy him lunch as compensation. It was just another three hour meaningless meeting during which I had written up three lots of staff supervision notes – everyone was impressed with the eagerness with which I was taking copious notes, prepared for the next meeting that was actually outcome focussed and sketched some ideas for my second A level art module – everyone doodles in meetings mine just happened to have a specific focus. Typically, no decisions were made at the conclusion of the meeting and three hours had been shaved off people's lives.

***

The gradual departure of the suits from the café suggests that the rain is easing or stopping. I wish the young woman all the best and depart. The rain has eased to a light drizzle and I decide to walk home. It has washed away all the street vendors and there is no sign of my woman with the baby or the man on the central reservation on Toledo who in the afternoon sells mangoes and oranges with the help of his school aged daughter. I am looking forward to a hot shower and a big mug of Yorkshire tea.

***

I have completed my weekly nit ritual. The nit lotion is nasty and removes the natural shine and softness out of my hair. So the weekly preventative nit treatment is followed by a weekly hot oil treatment to repair the damage. This isn't vanity – it's just that the scarecrow like appearance is a little too shocking even for me. I take my big mug of tea and tuck myself up in my sleeping bag on the sofa – the house feels damp and cold and we have no heating. As I sip my tea I realise that I am tired with a capital K. Given the early start this morning and tomorrow morning, I will treat myself to a chill out evening and an early night. I will not concede to a game of scrabble as my brain will let me down. As I doze I think about my weekly routine; work with street children four mornings a week, rich children one day a week and Spanish lessons four afternoons a week. I think I will reduce the lessons to three afternoons a week as I rather enjoyed having an afternoon to myself. The weekends are free for socialising and rambling. I would like to add and watching live football on Sundays but the league has just concluded with El Nacional winning and will not start again until the New Year.

I have been asleep for over an hour when Ben comes in, wakes me up and calls me a part-timer. He tells me that he has a present for me and hands me a copy the Guardian cryptic crossword puzzle. He gets himself a drink and tells me that he is off to the hammock for a snooze and to wake him up in half an hour. Yep, he's knackered too. I decide to deal with my e-mails and search the Internet for cartoon characters that might appeal to the children. I wake Ben up at about 8pm and inspired to do the crossword we crack a few clues. At 8.30pm I turn in as my brain can no longer think in the language of cryptic clues. I give Ben permission to drag me out of bed kicking and screaming if there is no sign of life by 6.30am. I would ask him to just leave a mug of fresh coffee on the bedside table as this is equally as effective but he knows that I can't trust him to make a descent cup of coffee or tea. I can't imagine wasting a Yorkshire teabag or having the wrong strength of coffee first thing in the morning.

Friday 18th November...

I am enjoying the view of the mountains whilst doing back crawl in the odd shaped school pool. The water is incredibly warm and it's nice to chill out at the end of a busy week. It has been another easy day and the children in the class are a pleasure to work with. One of my favourites is Pascal because he is exceptionally bright and achieves with very little effort. He is friends with a couple of other bright kids and between them they can be quite mischievous – it is interesting to watch all the things they get up to behind the teacher's back. I met Pascal's mother at the bonfire night and she made me feel very welcome. She immediately worked out that my parents must be from India and went on to tell me that she had spent a few years in Pakistan and that her eldest son was born there. I asked if she had learnt the language at which point she laughed and said her one and only word – thank you. I commented that it was an important one to know which made her laugh louder. We exchanged our cultural heritage and I found that hers was a right mishmash – including a bit of Egyptian. After 20 leisurely lengths I drag myself out of the pool into the cold air and make a dash towards the changing rooms. By the time I get showered and changed Ben's meeting will have finished. We will then head to the restaurant with Tamara to meet a group of teachers for a meal.

During the meal Ben and I mention our crazy plan to conquer Cotopaxi at Christmas. Tamara is interested in joining us. Clare and Woody advise that we do some serious training and invite all three of us for breakfast and a ramble up the mountain behind the school. We all accept.

Saturday 19th November...

Tamara and I are immersed in a deep and meaningful conversation whilst walking up the mountain behind the rest of the group. We're at the back because we're both struggling to breath. Tamara has genetically small lungs and I still can't stop coughing – I should not have neglected taking my drugs for the past few days. We've skipped past the usual superficial chit chat and are contemplating levels of enlightenment and how these are attained. We discuss how self awareness can lead to an inner rootedness and an inner stillness. We talk about the sandstorms of life that cloud the path to the inner stillness and how at these times it is easy to become uprooted and get caught in the eye of the storm. We concur that it is often the storms of life that strengthen the inner sanctum and lead to greater enlightenment. We pontificate the factors that contribute to inner wealth and inner impoverishment and ask ourselves if by becoming cash poor we can become life rich and how a healthy balance can be reached. By the end of the ramble we have covered many related subjects and found that we are on a similar wavelength. Ben comments that we seemed to be deep in conversation. I just nod my head.

***

We head back to Quito in time for Ben's rugby practice. On the way we stop at Mega Maxi for the weekly shop. I offer to cook an Indian meal on Sunday and really fancy cooking some okra or ladies fingers to compliment the chicken and lentil dishes. I have no joy at Mega Maxi so opt for the aubergines instead. I've offered to teach Ben some basic dishes so that he can enjoy the genuine article without relying on pastes. Ben drops me off at home and as usual we arrange to meet at the restaurant after the training.

Monday 21st November...

I'm no expert in the area of nits but I guess shaving the buggers off is as good a remedy as any – certainly cheaper than nit lotion. This is the drastic solution that greets me as I enter the dining room this Monday morning. All the boys are hairless – it's an invasion of the skin heads. Thankfully the remedy has not been applied to any of the girls – some religious or cultural norm has probably saved them. Breakfast has not yet finished and Michael as always is sitting with the children. His hair is growing like the thick ivy in my garden and could do with a little pruning – I'm surprised that Scary Nun didn't pin him down as well. As I join him, I comment, 'You've been spared.'

He laughs and tells me that yesterday the boys were lined up and shaved one by one. We don't even bother entering into a dialogue about children's rights as it would be futile. Scanning the room I notice that Jacson and Jairo are missing. I quizzically look at Michael who replies that they are washing their clothes and are not allowed to eat breakfast until the chore is done. As we wait for the children to finish their breakfast, Michael tells me that he is unhappy living at the project. The nuns have threatened to lock him out if he is not back by 9.00pm which is stopping him from socialising with his friends. They are even unhappy about him attending his music rehearsals as it means that they have to do the chores with the children. And they are now expecting him to get up with the children at 6.30am. Unfortunately, he has told them about his fencing lessons and they are not happy with this hobby either.

Jokingly I say, 'You might need to defend yourself so don't give it up.'

He replies, 'Do you think?'

Laughing I comment, 'Is that German humour?'

Our laughter is infectious as the children start laughing too. The teacher and social worker simply give us disapproving frowns. Suddenly two wet and rather guilty looking boys make their appearance at the doorway to the dining room – they clearly turned their punishment into a play opportunity.

As they sit at our table I quietly say, 'You weren't suppose to wash the clothes you're wearing.'

A couple of minutes later Iki arrives and asks, 'what's going on?'

I reply, 'You know, the usual madness.'

Her jaw drops as her eyes photograph each of the shaved heads. Even the teacher concedes a smile. I see Scary Nun heading at great speed towards the kitchen and suggest we beat a hasty retreat downstairs – we don't wait to find out what she wants. The children follow us down. As it is 9.30 we agree to not have a break today and to run through until 10.30. Standing by the white board Iki and I discuss the children. Over the weeks we have discovered what works for each child. Jacson learns best in short spurts – every morning we teach him for 20 minutes and then allow him to do activity based work. His has moved on from colouring cartoon characters to making mobiles from stars. I have gone from being a cartoonist to drawing stars on white card that Jacson cuts out, colours and glues to bits of string. Jairo will do maths for fun and is able to do simple addition. The first time he had to add two numbers that totalled greater than 10 he had two children holding up their hands as he counted. Now he is starting to add easy numbers mentally. In respect of the literacy we have reached an impasse as we suspect that he has dyslexia. He frequently writes some letters back to front and at times does the same with the numbers. We do not have the expertise to teach him, although we are trying to find ways to help him distinguish between the b and d and p and q. He and Jacson are still negotiating the basis of their friendship but I suspect that this morning's punishment helped to create a bond. Iki is frustrated that Antonia has not moved beyond doing tiny spirals, despite introducing her to different shapes. With a smile on my face I point out that she at least is using different colours. Today she is making her presence known and has hummed incessantly since entering the room.

Even Jacson has commented, 'Esta loca,' – She's mad.

Our plan is to ignore it and pretend that it's not bothering us. The pressure cooker is frustrated and Iki asks him to carry on with his work. Some days he works and other days he doesn't even enter the classroom. He still needs help to deal with his anger but I know that he will never get it. We have accepted our baby sitting role in respect of Henry. Generally he does behave and it's hard not to have a soft spot for him. He is developing good fine motor control skills as we get him to sit and draw every day. Naila is lovely and many people's favourite. She lives at the project during the week and goes home at weekends – it is rumoured that her mother is a sex worker. It is clear that she does receive some positive nurturing from her mother. For a five year old she writes incredibly neatly and we now have her writing the alphabet. She is more reticent to actually learn it but we keep chipping away. These are now the core group of children in the first session – others have come and gone. We turn to the wall that is now virtually covered with the children's work. Those that have moved on have left something of themselves – their presence here will be remembered in some small way. Julia's scribbles are amongst the works of art produced by the children. I suggest to Iki that it's time to start decorating the opposite wall.

Thirty minutes later Antonia is still humming and even the children are amazed at her accomplishment. The expression of disbelief on Iki's face is a picture. We stare at each other and know that we need a distraction to stop ourselves from mimicking the Edvard Munch scream. The distraction arrives in the form of a rag doll child bursting through the classroom door with the teacher. She is wearing rags and a hair style crafted by Edward Scissorhands. The teacher tells us that she is called Anita, sits her down and leaves. Anita is disabled and has no decipherable verbal communication. She has an intense stare and a manic laugh. We give her some plain paper and a handful of colouring pencils and watch in horror as she violently breaks the tip of every one and then rips the paper into small pieces. This act is followed up with the manic laugh.

Iki's first response is, 'I finish in four days.'

I reply, 'Perhaps destructive art activities will meet her needs,' and conclude that my remaining few weeks could be a bit of a nightmare. In the background the incessant humming continues. Fortunately it's 10.15 and time for El Patito Feo – Jacson's hope has been restored. Iki reads to the tune of humming.

The second group has changed since last week. Isabel our little escapee has gone but this time legitimately through the front gates with her aunt. We will miss her and especially her expressive face – the change in expression from puzzlement to sudden enlightenment never ceased to amuse us or the other group members. Sofia a 9 year old has taken her place. It is clear that she is another bright spark. As we are about to start work with the second group we are told that all the children are needed by the social worker – except the disabled ones. With nothing to do I propose that we go for a coffee. On the way out we get stopped by Scary Nun and are told to shower the disabled girls. Staring at the nun with a big smile on my face I want to point out that even the children say please and thank you – although admittedly this task has taken us three weeks. I want to say, 'What big eyes you have.' The nun has lit Iki's furious fuse and she is clenching her fists and gritting her teeth. I grab her arm, smile at the Scary Nun and head towards the carpentry. Here we collect Antonia and Anita – after showering them we leave. We say our goodbyes in Mariscal and agree to conduct the post-mortem over dinner tonight. The poor guys are in for an earful.

***

I'm strolling back along 12 de Octubre from La Torre Eifel after my first and final private English lesson with Santiago. After the hour I told Santiago that he didn't need English lessons but simply English practice. I could speak English with him once a week but at $10 per hour this would ultimately be very expensive for him. He admitted that he wasn't the richest of restaurant owners but did want to improve his English as he had plans to go to Europe next year. He wants to visit London and his brother in Paris – hence the French sentiment. We explored how he could access English speaking groups. I learnt that his wife is actively involved in a multi-national church where there are English speakers but he isn't a church goer. I wanted to refrain from suggesting going to church simply to practice his English but he was failing to make the connection so I proposed attending church. I offered to search the web and get him some information on cheap accommodation in London.

As I turn into Madrid I see that all my usual human landmarks are doing business. The medicine man on the corner of Octubre and Madrid always seems to do a sterling trade in the mornings as commuters stop on route and drink all sorts of potions. Business is usually slower in the afternoons. The shoe shine man and boy are also busier in the mornings than at this time of day. Further up Madrid I spot my sweet woman, say hello and buy some sweets. Her baby daughter is now able to stand unaided. As I turn into Toledo I see that the fruit and newspaper man is missing. As I continue to walk up I spot him crouched in a corner, in front of the corner shop. He is making up tubular bags of mangoes that he sells in the afternoons. He really does have a good location as he catches the peak time traffic both in the mornings and afternoons. Turning into Pontevedra I smile as I see the rusty Darshan Singh sign. I still haven't popped in to say hello. As I walk past the neighbours barred gate I say hello to the maid – we greet each other most mornings and afternoons. The next few hours are going to be busy as I need to get all my work done before going out for dinner.

Tuesday 22nd November...

Today the atmosphere is relaxed. All the children know that it is Iki's birthday and that they will be treated to birthday cake. It's only 10.00am and Jacson wants to know when they will get the cake. I simply say, 'Despues.'

Without much success we have tried to teach this group how to tell the time. They have no concept of time and their lives are driven by the routine of breakfast, lunch and dinner. Teaching today is futile and we are doing fun activities like colouring, cutting out and playing dominoes. Antonia is quietly drawing spirals – there is no humming today. Whilst the children are occupied we talk positively about our night out – we went to a Mongolian restaurant where you could eat and drink as much as you wanted for $10. Anita causes me to stop mid sentence when she walks in wearing Julia's khaki pinafore dress. Julia wasn't even allowed to take her one and only dress – the dress that she liked to point to every time she wore it as if to say, 'Look at me in my dress.'

I give Anita some paper and a pair of scissors. I figured that cutting the paper with a pair of scissors might keep her occupied a bit longer than simply tearing it with her bare hands. She starts cutting away and soon there are snowflakes of paper on the table and floor. It's nearly 10.20 and we tell the kids that it's break time. Iki and I pop out to the corner shop to collect the cake. I pay for the cake as I believe that no one should buy their own birthday cake. We return with two 18" diameter cakes and find that all the children are patiently waiting in the dining room. We cut up the cake and hand it out. Before tucking in the children are asked to sing happy birthday. Iki had prepared little bags of sweets for all the children – it reminds me of Lord of the Rings and Frodo giving out gifts on his birthday. As well as sweets the girls' bags contain hair bands. I watch as the girls replace their elastic hair bands with bright coloured hair bands. This little gesture means so much to them. Iki asks me about the nuns. I suggest that she leaves them some cake as well – without any additives!

Sunday 27th November...

We have just started walking from the Teleférico when Ben asks, 'Have you remembered your inhaler?'

Clare expresses my thoughts for me by saying, 'Your reminder is a bit late.'

I laugh and say, 'Yes I have.'

Five of us decided to make the most of the weather and walk to the top from the Teleférico – this chairlift was not here on my last trip. At first everyone is walking and chatting away but this soon gives way to silence as the ascent becomes increasingly challenging. I am in need of a break when I hear a distant voice calling my name. I'm convinced I must be hearing things but feel reassured when Ben says, 'It's for you.'

I turn round to find Santiago and his son, who is also named Santiago, trying to catch us up. I introduce him to Ben and the group and explain that they are my friends. Santiago kindly invites us all to have free burgers at his restaurant. I thank him for his gesture and ask how the English is progressing. I am impressed to hear that he has made contact with English speakers at his church. He thanks me for my advice and tells Ben that I am a good person – under my breath I utter, 'Deep-down we all are.'

After a few minutes of exchanging pleasantries we continue walking. After an hour or so we are standing looking at the scree slope that we are about to ascend. It is steep and long. As we start walking again the conversation is used as sparingly as the oxygen.

'How are the legs?' I ask Ben.

'Jellified,' he replies.

'And yours?'

'Hollow,' is my single word answer.

A little further up Ben says, 'And the asthma?'

'Well drugged,' I reply.

'And your breathing?' I ask.

'Laboured,' is Ben's monosyllabic reply.

Jokingly, I offer him my inhaler. Tamara is also on this trip but on this occasion she is totally focussed on the walking. Intermittently, she stops to photograph every new flower that she sees – she did this on the last walk as well. After many, many stops we all collapse at the top and Clare treats us to Cadbury's milk chocolate. It has been a hard climb and Ben and I know that we need more practice before we tackle Cotopaxi.

Sitting on top of Rucu Pichincha, engulfed by the panorama of mountains, I realise that it is the last weekend of November and time is passing like a tide receding into the distant horizon. Like me everyone is lost in their own thoughts and the silence is heavenly. I reflect on yesterday's visit to the children's project – I took Ben, Caz and Saskia. It was more chaotic than usual as it had all my children, children that reside at the project but attend school during the day – these I rarely see – and a group of lads that had been caught stealing and brought to the project by the police. There was a right carry on in the main courtyard and from what I gathered the fathers were negotiating the release of their sons – like I always thought a children's prison! Michael was there and told me that it had been mad all morning. I introduced him to Ben and left them to talk about rugby as Michael was keen to join the team.

I'm not sure what Ben thought about the project. I've deduced that he likes to share his thoughts on matters in his own time – the only danger is that you could grow old waiting! Even threatening to beat him up doesn't get a response and he just laughs. I know that the kids took to him, especially Jacson and José – who Ben commented had the build of a miniature rugby player. I know that he was amused by the wide rimmed sunhat worn by the senior nun under her wimple. Caz and Saskia were absorbed by the six month old baby and wanted to take her home – the maternal hormones were pumping into the atmosphere and I wasn't sure whose needs were being met. I've learnt not to form too strong a bond with the children as this is unfair on them – volunteers come and volunteers go and bonds are formed and broken on a frequent basis which cannot be healthy for the kids. This baby girl was the second baby that had appeared at the project over the last week. The first was a bonny little baby boy who was found abandoned on the street. He was very well dressed and had received some good care. He arrived on Wednesday morning but was moved to a baby unit by Thursday. I knew this baby too would be gone by Monday morning. At least the babies have a glimmer of hope of adoption and a good family life. Scary Nun managed to keep up appearances – she told my visitors that volunteers were really valued and even embraced a couple of the children. If only Iki could have witnessed this. But it didn't last and she was soon telling my friends how much money she needed and shouting at the children. On the way out Michael said that he was glad to be working with me – it will be a new journey. I will miss Iki and will always value the time we spent together. I accept that just like the children the volunteers will also come and go. Journeys and lives will be shared and enriched.

Saturday 3rd December...

By now it's well past 8.30am – my alarm resonated in my inner ears at least 10 minutes ago – and I am still lying in bed with my eyes shut. In a half-willed attempt to motivate myself into action I stick my arm out and reluctantly draw back one of the curtains. I open my eyes to find the sun smiling invitingly in a pale blue sky – typical! I still don't want to leap out of my warm bed. What would work is a mug of fresh black coffee – each sip gently kicking the brain cells into a state of submission and alertness. Sadly, Ben hasn't mastered the skill to make the perfect mug.

Instead of moving, I give free reign to my brain. Another week of my life has passed away – second by second, minute by minute, hour by hour, day by day. How have I spent this precious resource? I think about the project and decide it was a time of growth and well spent. Not surprisingly, Michael and I worked like a perfectly blended masala – or maybe it was a bit more like a Punch and Judy show. The tone for the week was set on Monday morning. I was just telling the children what to do, when from the corner of my eye I caught Michael shoving my pocket dictionary into his trouser pocket. I stopped talking, turned towards him and asked, 'Que haces?'

He looked up and said, 'You need a big pocket for this,' and fell about laughing.

It shouldn't have been funny but at the time it really was and I could not help but laugh – I could see his point as it is A5 size, three inches thick and yet is called a pocket dictionary! I grabbed the dictionary and gently bashed him across the head. The laughter was contagious and the children joined in not knowing why we were laughing. I looked at Michael and said, 'You explain the joke to them.'

He looked at the children and simply said, 'Este dictionario es muy grande.'

I shook my head and jokingly uttered the word, 'Pathetic,' before suggesting we try and teach. Day by day we got by with a little help from the children, our limited but fast developing Spanish, the pocket dictionary, a bit of pictionary and an enormous sense of humour. The second group of children were very entertained as Michael and I formulated the correct sentences and argued over verb conjugation. They were all quite happy to help out. I think everyone's lives were enriched by the whole experience but I'm not sure who learnt the most!

However, on Thursday morning Scary Nun made an appearance. As usual Michael and I were laughing and just making our way down to the classrooms when she came charging towards us with a wagging finger. Within seconds she had invaded our personal space – intuitively we moved shoulder to shoulder – and the wagging finger was in my face, then Michael's and then in mid air. I had to stop myself from nodding at the same rate as the finger. She babbled on and I simply shrugged my shoulders pretending not to understand. She turned to Michael and asked him to interpret.

Michael turned his head towards me and said, 'But you understand.'

'I know that, you know that but she doesn't,' I replied.

The poor lad started to interpret, 'You must work all day, help the girls to shower and wash the clothes with the children.'

'That is one well accomplished frown. Is she aware that it takes more muscles to frown than to smile?' I observe.

'What?'

'Look at the frown and those big scary eyes,' I replied.

Not understanding my comment he continued, 'You must work until 2 O'clock.'

Rhetorically I asked, 'If I smile do you think she will smile back at me?'

Totally confused Michael said, 'What do you want me to say to her?'

'That the words please and thank you are really nice words. I'm just joking. I will speak to her myself,' I told him.

I looked directly at Scary Nun's big eyes – she now had both hands firmly on her sizeable hips – and told her in English that loads of grey strands had escaped the wimple this morning making her scarier than normal. Then I reverted to Spanish and politely told her that I could not stay as I had Spanish lessons in the afternoon.

I wanted to add, 'And I'm not here next Monday or Tuesday either as I will be busy celebrating la fiesta de Quito,' but I decided not to push my luck.

Incredulously, she told me to change my classes. I told her that it would not be possible. She was not amused and stormed off. Michael looked at me and asked what I said about the hair. The rest of the morning was spoilt as Anna Gabriella was forced to work in the kitchen and miss her lessons – I protested but to no avail. Interestingly, it was the social worker who was behind the decision – the teacher had conceded.

That afternoon, I met some fellow students at the Coffee House Company café. Thursday afternoons have become my chill out time – time to spend with fellow travellers and time to explore the city. After a drink, two of us headed off to the Guayasamin museum. According to the museum information, Oswaldo Guayasamin dedicated his art to confronting the cruelties and injustices of modern society. His canvases do bring to life strong, powerful images that convey raw emotion – pain, suffering and despair – the depths of which can only be imagined by the observer. These images capture the despair of people that I see every day – the poor, the disabled and the destitute. Perhaps as a contrast someone should capture the emotions of the rich, those destined for great things. What would these images look like?

***

Thinking about the rich, the day at Ben's school went smoothly and the children were as easy as ever to work with. Apart from doing the odd jobs, I am now helping to make props for the Christmas play – yet another performance. Unlike the project there is an Aladdin's cave of resources. I managed to get permission to photocopy some of the resources for the children at the project – I want to collate some resources for Michael and the new volunteers – and take some green and white card for the first group. I want them to cut out and decorate a Christmas tree that will take pride of place on the remaining white classroom wall. At the end of an easy day I went for a swim – I could never tire of the surrounding mountains – whilst Ben played tennis.

***

It's nearly 9.15 and definitely time for coffee and a leisurely breakfast before watching some live English football on TV. Why is it that some football teams are like Marmite – you either hate them or love them? If you hate them, you love to see them lose and if you love them you hate to see them lose.

After appreciating Ben's cooked breakfast of bacon, eggs, tomatoes and toast I claim the sofa and turn on the TV – I'm still in my pyjamas and dressing gown. I'm watching the live football whilst Ben is reading the commentary of the same match on the computer – in between reading the commentary on the Palace match of course. The situation is comical as I see the goals or near goals before the information appears as text on the computer – but this doesn't persuade Ben to just watch the live football match instead. 'And you call me nuts,' I comment.

Momentarily, he turns his head towards the television and then back to the computer screen. I'm more interested in the next match – Man Utd. I convince Ben that we have time to watch the first half of the game before heading off to his rugby tournament. The Quito rugby team is playing against the team from Quayaquil in a cup tournament. A group of girlies are going along to support the lads. I know nothing about rugby but Paul's mum has agreed to explain the game as it is played.

It's the end of the first half and within five minutes I am showered and dressed and ready to head off to the meet the crowds at Dos Argentinos – Ben tells me that he is impressed. Much to my delight the second half of the game is being shown and I grab a seat inside the restaurant whilst everyone is getting themselves organised. Even little Jesse's attempts to distract me by doing karate chops and kicks all down my chin don't work. Just as a tornado of a second goal is scored, Ben drags me away from the TV and onto the coach. Foolishly he sits next to me and gets a blow by blow account of the goals.

***

This rugby lark is painful if nothing else. I feel sorry for the poor blonde haired lad whose head is repeatedly kissing the ground – I cringe on his behalf every time he is decked and covered by an incredible mass of bodies. I want to offer him an ice pack. Some of the spectators are so engrossed in the game that they too are running up and down the sidelines with the players and shouting all sorts of advice. In between selling beers and soft drinks, I join in but mainly to keep warm. Suddenly, the game becomes interesting as one of our lads catches the ball, dashes down the length of the field and slides over the line. 'So that's a touchdown then,' I say to Paul's mum.

'No dear, it's a try,' is her polite reply. 'And that is a conversion,' she tells me as the ball passes between the two tall posts of the letter H.

I still can't remember whether this is rugby league or rugby union but haven't the nerve to ask again. As the game approaches its conclusion – our team is winning – the referee storms off the pitch and gets into his car. I comment to Saskia, 'I assume that's not part of the game.'

She confirms that it isn't and explains that the linesman has upset the referee and he has quit. This has certainly made the game a whole lot more fascinating and entertaining – it can only happen here. I watch as events unfold. Players on both teams try and talk to the referee and linesman. The linesman is unrepentant and the referee is having none of it and drives off in his four by four with his dogs and children – the clouds of dust lingering in the air adds the comical icing to this very comical 20 minutes. With a gentlemanly handshake, the two sides agree that the cup should go to the leading team. So Quito win, but it seems like a strange victory. I sell all the players drinks to help them get over the shock of the situation and in doing so make enough money to cover the expenses – I don't quite know how I ended up as bursar. After the match we return home to get ready for the evening.

***

Ben is looking down at me, which is the norm, but at least he hasn't taken to resting his arms on my head. Standing on the roof of this small packed bus, he is simultaneously shaking his head and smiling. In the short time that I have known him, I have concluded that sensible Ben is not a huge risk taker. So accepting the Chiva challenge this evening is a little out of character. As the bus starts moving, over the loud music I yell, 'At least if we die we can claim that we were led out by a brass band, even though it is to the tune of the Ecuadorian national anthem.'

Ben just gives me the, 'You are definitely nuts,' look. Within a few minutes my words almost turn into a real life drama as the bus brakes and everyone lurches forward. I grab onto Ben who is sensibly gripping the precariously attached handrail. I find myself staring into the blood shot eyes of the drunken drummer. Not surprisingly, he stops drumming. He reaches into his coat pocket and pulls out a bottle of the local lighter fuel. He offers me a swig. I find myself politely declining the offer, whilst being pulled backwards by Ben. The drummer takes a large gulp of the liquid and resumes his drumming. Over the loud music, I hear Ben yell, 'You okay?' I stick out my thumb.

The crushing is becoming rhythmic – to the left, to the right, forward, back and repeat. Every few minutes everyone is ducking to avoid either the overhead cables or the branches of the trees. People seem happy under the influence of the alcohol that is being passed around every few minutes. Too eager to absorb the atmosphere, I decline the offers of cheap wine and spirit. Below me the streets are full of people celebrating the fiesta de Quito. Music is emanating from all directions, from the street bands, from the roof tops of the other Chivas cruising the streets, as well as from bars and houses. At every set of traffic lights more people jump onto our bus, which seems to have taken on the characteristics of a Tardis. Amidst the smell of burning meat, I can smell sweet aromas but cannot identify the food. The smells trigger my hunger juices. Behind me, I hear Paul's mother shout, 'Bueno, bueno.'

I turn my head and smile. Two seconds later, she offers her glasses to the branch of a tree and simply says, 'Never mind' and slaps me on my back. She is clearly enjoying herself and willing to give new experiences a go.

At the end of the Chiva experience, we get dropped off just outside the Mongolian restaurant in Mariscal. Squeezing through the crowds, we enter the restaurant where we join the rest of the rugby players and their supporters for food and drink – a night out with rugby players is the third new experience of the day. Suitably replete, I sit back with my second blue coloured cocktail and observe the crowds. As the night unfolds, the alcohol is doing what it does best – removing the barriers of inhibition. From across the large, open plan restaurant I watch as some of the rugby players stagger onto the long wooden tables and start to salsa. Not to be outdone, the group from the neighbouring table follow suit. From a distance, Ben catches my attention and sticks out his thumb whilst mouthing, 'OK.' I nod my head. Even he has been consuming alcohol but not to the point of dancing on tables – now that would be an unlikely sight. On another table, the other teachers from the rugby are continuing to do what groups of any profession do when they congregate – talk shop. I chuckle as I watch the girlfriends of the rugby players protect their men from other women. There is almost an animalistic aggression behind the pretentious smiles and the beautifully painted faces. My quiet enjoyment is suddenly interrupted by three of the rugby players from Guayaquil who have joined me at my table. They all light up, unintentionally blow smoke in my direction and introduce themselves in pigeon English. Not amused, I gently take a cigarette from the mouth of one man and extinguish it on the inside of an empty glass and return it to him. His eyes carefully follow my deliberately slow actions. I then stare at the other two, who obligingly put out their cigarettes. Even before asking my name one of the men interjects with, 'You have boyfriend?'

I simply stare at him, smile and say, 'Do you have girlfriends in Guayaquil or here?' – momentarily I look around to see if I am about to be savaged by three women on heat; I'm quite partial to my hair and face.

They respond with frowns, turn towards each other and start conversing in Spanish. They argue over whether or not I have a boyfriend, my likely age, which of them I actually fancy and whether I would be going to the nightclub. I find the conversation faintly amusing and burst out laughing. Unfortunately, I give the game away, as one of the guys asks, 'Habla Español?'

My silence forces him to revert to English. 'How you say, you misteriosa?'

I laugh and say, 'There's nowt mysterious about me lad, just ask my fish,' knowing full well that they would not understand. As Ben approaches, I decide to put them out of their misery and tell them in plain English that I do not have boyfriend, I am not in my twenties – I wanted to add that the alcohol has blurred their vision but decided that it would not be unnecessary – and I don't do nightclubs.

Towering over the men, Ben says, 'Had enough?'

One of the men asks, 'Novio?'

I reply, 'No es mi novio, es mi amigo Ben.'

I turn to Ben – who is smiling and as usual quite happy to let me do the explaining – and say, 'It's been entertaining but I've certainly had enough. Let's walk home so that we can take in the street fiesta.'

Sunday 11th December...

With every step up Guagua Pichincha I am uttering the words, 'It does not hurt, it does not hurt.' However, as I walk, I can feel my feet throbbing and I desperately want to stop and scratch. With gritted teeth I resist all temptation and curse the Deet immune mosquito type insects that mauled my ankles, feet and legs at yesterday's wedding. Fearlessly, the little bastards feasted on my body before my very eyes and left behind contrails of blood. Overnight, my feet underwent a metamorphosis and this morning I woke up to two balloons that did not want to fit into my walking boots – so I am in my runners. I blame myself for deciding to dance in bare feet. Despite the pain, I know that the training must go on as we will be climbing Cotopaxi on December 27th.

Ben, although sympathetic, cannot resist smiling as he hears my mutterings – he, like the other men, was fine in his protective wedding suit. Perhaps if they had all been wearing kilts – no, let's not go there. 'Do your feet still hurt?' he asks.

I reply, 'Just a little.'

We talk about the wedding and agree that it was perhaps one of the fastest civil services we had ever attended – the clerk was running so late that she whizzed through the process, introduced the couple as man and wife and took off. But at least it did actually happen given all the bureaucratic hurdles – the red tape in this country would rival that in India. The school grounds provided the perfect setting for both the service and the reception – the cook put on such a superb buffet that even I helped myself to a second serving. I tell Ben that his speech was very good and no one would have guessed that it was drafted only hours before it was due to be delivered. My comment receives a grin.

As we continue walking, we take up occupancy in our own private worlds. I am still thinking about the wedding. I smile as I think about the garter. Instead of throwing her flowers over her head, Ximena explained that she would throw her garter – I'm not sure if this is customary or whether Ximena made it up! With gold laden champagne in hand, I decided to watch the 'ritual' from a safe distance. All the single women gathered behind her before she cast her garter into the air – Paula caught it. Ximena then asked all the bachelors to line up and chose one to roll the garter onto Paula's thigh using only his mouth. Ben was the victim but through the flushes of embarrassment he fulfilled his obligation – and I caught the whole experience on video. What I also captured was the look of envy on two women's faces – the green tan was not caused by the mid afternoon sun. If Ben only knew – maybe I will tell him one day.

Breathlessly (joke) we reach the top of Guagua – Guagua is the younger crater of Pichincha – but the mist beats us to it and denies us the view. We hang about on the ridge in the hope that the strong winds will brush it aside but after 10 minutes of shivering we conclude that it is a futile exercise – at least my feet are now chilled to the point of numbness and are no longer throbbing. On the way down we discuss what to do tonight – Paul's parents are spending a few days with us so that the newly weds can have some time alone. Ben suggests testing the cooker with a roast dinner – I readily agree with the idea. Teasingly, he talks about enriching the taste buds with 'A nice bit of beef,' – but I know that he will not cook the sacred cow as he hasn't even had beef in the house since my arrival. As we near the car we look back to find the mountain framed by nothing but blue sky. 'Nature has its own sense of humour,' I mutter to no one in particular.

Wednesday 14th December...

It is a glorious summer type day and my penultimate working day at the project. The last two weeks have jogged along with the usual ups and downs. Today, all the young captives are playing in Parque Carolina and my ears are enjoying the music of their laughter and shouting. My nostrils are absorbing the smell of freshly cut grass – the sneezing storm is slowly brewing and no doubt my eyes will soon start itching as my hypersensitivity disorder kicks off. No, I am not day dreaming in the middle of a Spanish lesson – the children really are in the park and annoyingly I do have a hypersensitivity disorder – mind over matter just hasn't worked. We are here thanks to Michael who secured some money from one of the German NGOs to pay for a trip to the butterfly farm. As the farm is situated within the park we decided to let the escapees run loose after the visit.

Now, sitting comfortably under the shade of a large tree, we are trying to make sense of Anita's behaviour. In the farm she moved her hand at such great speed that she caught a butterfly in flight. Michael and I both witnessed the incident and immediately looked at each other for confirmation of what we had seen. We then rescued the half crushed admiral from her clenched fist – whilst she laughed manically. After nearly three weeks, the only thing we have deduced with certainty is that Anita's unpredictable behaviour is completely unpredictable. When helping her to wash her clothes, Michael has heard her sing nursery rhymes and thinks she suffered some sort of head injury as a young child.

We use the opportunity to review the progress made by the other children. The first group is busy decorating the second white wall in the classroom. Jacson has stuck a big green card board cut out of a Christmas tree to the wall and has been slowly decorating it with Jairo – a friendship has developed but sadly it will be short-lived as Jairo will soon return home. Jairo's maths has improved but he still struggles with language – bs are still interchanged with ds and ps with qs. Antonia draws her perfect spirals and nothing more – she still occasionally hums all the way through a lesson – and I'm none the wiser on how to engage with her other than through the occasional hug when she is upset and drawing spirals with her. Naila has learnt some of the alphabet and now recognises some words but still tries to get out of doing any work by smiling sweetly but Michael does not give in. Well fed Henry is just starting to string one or two words together. Even the pressure cooker has calmed down to the point where the furniture is no longer used as projectiles. New children have joined this core group for short periods of time – many have appeared and disappeared within a day and none have left an impression.

The second group now consists of Maria, Myra, José, Anna Gabriella and a new girl called Careena. The bright and determined Sophia stayed only a short while. Intellectually, she and Anna Gabriella sparred off each other beautifully. These children have excelled and their A4 notebooks contain pages and pages of work. With pride they look at their work and are able to see their own progress. They are no longer afraid to ask questions, to make mistakes and to demand more. We laugh as we recall the day when the children kept on demanding more and more words during a spelling test. By the time I reached the 25th word I had to say, 'No mas' as I didn't know any more words for items of clothing. Just for kicks Michael had joined in with the children and kept chanting, 'Uno mas.' Language is not a barrier when it comes to humour.

We reflect on the highs and lows. Teaching and especially teaching in a new language has been fun and challenging – neither of us spoke a word before we arrived in the country. The children have certainly found us entertaining – the laughter levels have at times reached the upper echelons and resulted in a reprimand. Even the encounters with the increasingly mythical Scary Nun have provided endless hours of amusement. Sadly, the lack of information for and communication with the volunteers by the staff and nuns has been a major source of frustration. As foreign volunteers it has been difficult to know what to do, what to say and how to respond to child discipline and the use of corporal punishment. 'I will miss you,' Michael tells me.

'Who wouldn't miss me,' I reply whilst maintaining a straight face.

We both fall about laughing and Michael says, 'You funny.'

I then reassure him that he will be okay as two new young volunteers will be joining the project. I know that he is very unhappy and really wants to leave the project. I feel powerless to do anything about it although I have asked Ben to look out for him once I leave.

We watch with delight as the children enjoy their freedom. Anna Gabriella comes towards us but seems unsure about joining us. With a big smile I wave her over and invite her to sit down with us. We both give her a big hug. It is little consolation for yesterday's mistreatment – despite my protests, the social worker forced the child to work in the kitchen and miss her lessons. I'm still angry because deep down I know that it is racism – the child slaves from morning until evening. I pull out a pen and writing pad and challenge her to a game of dot to dot. The kids love playing this game as well as noughts and crosses and I know that it is something that they will continue to do – my lasting legacy! Michael is distracted by one of the other children. As we play the game, I realise that we are both playing to let the other win. We settle for a draw and then play a few games of noughts and crosses. I offer to cover the lesson that she missed yesterday. Without hesitation and with a big smile she says, 'Si.'

Within 25 minutes we have covered the 2, 3 and 4 times table, the list of words, the planets, galaxies and the universe. Half way through, the social worker invites herself over. The victorious smirk of yesterday is wiped clean off as she sees what I am doing – she retreats without comment. Covertly,

Anna Gabriella smiles at me – she's not daft! I write out the list of words for the morning for I am determined to have her in the class.

Intuitively, Jacson knows when it is sweet time – I started this ritual the week Iki left – and walks over with his hand wide open. I always let Jacson, Anna Gabriella and Antonia take two as these are the children that always lose out. He takes his usual two – always the chocolate flavoured ones, says thank you and skips off. Today he is happy. I offer the bag to Anna Gabriella who takes one – she prefers the strawberry ones but does try the other flavours. She only ever takes a second sweet when invited to do and she is the only child who never rushes in to grab a sweet but waits until everyone else has taken one. Unprompted, she always says thank you. How can the nuns not see the wonderful qualities in this child? She is a credit to her family and I pray that soon she will be reunited with them as the sadness is starting to overpower her natural happiness. Suddenly, like goldfish to fishflakes, all the children are surrounding me with their grabbing hands. Anna Gabriella has moved to one side.

I take the bag and run off with twenty kids in tow. 50 metres later and out of breath, I stop and offer the sweets. Once the children have helped themselves I offer the sweets to the volunteers and adults. Both the social worker and teacher decided to accompany us on the free trip – but I fear that the social worker will not see the difference that it has made to the children. I offer them the bag to symbolically restore my own inner balance that had been disturbed in yesterday's storm.

Saturday 24th December…

Distant voices are pulling me away from the depths of this subconscious place and bringing me into consciousness. Against my will, I respond. 'Why I am hearing voices?' I mutter to myself. I feel for my watch amongst the clutter on the bedside table. It is just before 7am. I'm confused – Ben didn't say anyone would be visiting this early in the morning. Still drowsy, I drag myself out of bed to investigate. I see Stuart sitting on the sofa in the living room. He is rocking to and fro whilst hugging himself and carrying even more tension than usual. I'm very confused as I remember saying goodbye to him last night. Seeking an explanation, I turn my head towards Ben, who is hovering near the dining table. Ben looks at Stuart. The silence is suddenly interrupted. 'I was mugged on the way to the taxi rank and the bastards took everything,' Stuart tells me.

I'm enlightened and suddenly very awake. I offer to put the kettle on and head towards the kitchen – I am of the opinion it is always best to gather one's thoughts to avoid saying something stupid. Ben follows me and explains that he didn't wake me up last night when Stuart returned to the house as I looked shattered when I turned in – he knew too well that Stuart would have kept me up half the night. I appreciate his consideration and say thanks. I must have been really tired as I slept through the whole episode. We concur that Stuart is in a state of shock and discuss what course of action needs to be taken. Ben has already arranged to drive him home. I offer to contact Caz and find out if the matter needs to be reported to the police.

Stuart walks into the kitchen and Ben leaves me to it. I make him a cup of tea – the great English remedy for all manner of ills – and offer him a hug which he accepts. As he drinks his tea, with tears he recounts what happened. On the way down to the taxi rank on Madrid, a car pulled up ahead of him and three black men got out and walked in his direction. As they approached him, they attacked him, punching him to the ground and grabbed his backpack and wallet. Through the thinning hair I can see the small cut and bruise on the top of his head. I notice the drops of dried blood on his beige sweat shirt. He tells me that at first he tried to fight back but resisted when he saw the shining metal of what he feared to be a gun. He expresses his powerlessness and failure to fight back. I'm sensing the fear and rage in his voice but know that he needs to go through these stages before accepting what happened and moving on. I suggest that he returns with Ben and phones home from our computer – I know that he is close to his family and hearing their voices might help. I advise him not to tell them about the incident until he has had time to digest it – problems away from home tend to take on a magnitude of their own. Intuitively, Ben comes through and I see them off.

Before phoning Caz, I make myself a cup of coffee – I wish I could go and sit by my fish pond. I sigh in disappointment as I curl up on the sofa. Last night's event was not the way I expected to end a fabulous week in the mountains. On Monday, we enjoyed the slow gradual trudge up Él Corazón, even though it was overcast and drizzly. We walked through farming land where we were greeted by the locals with the words, 'Feliz navidad, un regalo por favor.' Sadly I had to disappoint them and say that we had no gifts. They responded with laughter. After Él Corazón we climbed Illiniza Norte, which is twinned with Illiniza Sur. This mountain really did test the lungs and legs. However, I'm likely to remember it more for the thunder storm that we experienced at the top. It was building up quickly as we ascended the last 100 metres and before we reached the top, we could hear the distant thunder and feel the tingling of lightning through our bodies. The bullet like hail hammered down on us as we found the metal cross that marked the very top – we decided not to touch this particular trig point. I laughed as I remembered comments made by friends – mountains to die on. As we were making our way back along the ridge Ben turned to me and said, 'Even your hair would stand on edge and make a great photo.'

Just in case he got any funny ideas, I quickly put my hands over my woollen hat – a photo of me with my shoulder length hair standing on end would no doubt end up on Ben's travel website with a caption along the lines of, 'The scary movie moment!' Sensibly, we abandoned the rocky ridge and descended via the scree slope before heading to the bright red refuge for shelter. As we entered the refuge the mountains vanished behind heavy cloud. Fortunately, within an hour we were graced with a photogenic sight of blue skies and snow covered mountains.

From these mountains we headed towards Quilotoa and walked around the beautiful emerald Laguana. By the time we completed the circuit the blue skies were replaced by heavy rain and strong winds. We encountered two foreign men who were the perfect advertisement for suitable mountain attire – dressed in designer jeans, t-shirts and trainers and with no protective gear! We rescued the shivering souls, loaned them dry fleeces and drove them back to the village.

We interspersed the training with some sightseeing including a trip to the famous Saquisilí market – a market or rather a collection of markets where you can buy everything from fruit and vegetables to livestock. Repeatedly, I was offered guinea pigs and rabbits. I was even offered a healthy looking goat – I wanted to explain that customs might object but instead declined the offer to buy the animal. One of my favourite moments was watching a woman with a very aged face trying on a brightly coloured, yellow and orange striped, woollen hat. She then tried several other hats but returned to the one that she had tried first of all – she was deriving great pleasure from simply stroking the soft wool. There was no mirror so she had no idea what it actually looked like. I wanted to tell her that it looked great. I asked if I could take her photograph – she allowed me to do so. It is a picture that I will treasure for a lifetime – this old woman, with very dark weathered skin, dressed in dark clothing, wearing a brightly coloured hat that lit up her face. From a distance I watched a group of men working some old fashioned, foot treadle sewing machines. Within a few moments they realised that I was watching and shooed me away. I spotted Ben as he discreetly snapped away. How can a white guy who towers most people by a foot seem so invisible – well he managed it and took some great photos.

After a week in the mountains, we arrived back home at about 8pm – having spent an hour in the madness of Friday night city traffic. We all grabbed a quick shower before enjoying a good feed at the local Chinese restaurant and reminiscing about the trip. As it was late we offered Stuart a mattress for the night but he was keen to get home and enjoy the comfort of his own bed. I suggested leaving his backpack as we could bring it over on Sunday. He declined the offer and set off at 10pm – I said goodnight, headed straight for my bed and surrendered my body to sleep. I'm glad that Ben didn't wake me up – already physically drained I don't think I was ready to be zapped of emotional energy as well.

Reflecting on the sequence of events, I can't help but conclude that Stuart's attack could have been prevented. Perhaps if he had stayed the night or perhaps if he had at least left his backpack he may not have attracted so much attention to himself. If only, if only, if only… Ironically, it was only a few weeks earlier, whilst walking back from a function held by Ecuador Volunteers, that Stuart and I were discussing safety at night. Stuart was firmly of the opinion that he would start worrying about personal safety if something actually happened to him. Maybe in the future he will exercise greater caution.

It's time to phone Caz. Caz tells me that the crime needs to be reported and offers to take Stuart to the relevant police station. I am grateful for her time as I know that she is busy cooking Christmas dinner for eight people for tonight. She invited us to Christmas dinner but we had already accepted an invitation from the teachers, so she kindly moved it to Christmas Eve. When Ben and Stuart return, we make the necessary arrangements and I offer to accompany Stuart and Caz to station.

***

It is late in the evening and we are back from our first Christmas dinner. We are slouching on the sofa and chatting about the day. The police station was a place of great activity but sadly a place of little progress. I entertained Jesse whilst Caz explained what had happened first to one police officer, then another and then a third. After 45 minutes Stuart was told to report the incident to a different station on Monday. 'Muggings happen, get over it,' perhaps best describes the attitude of the police officer concerned. In reality what can the police do? Sadly, muggings are a reality. In between reporting the incident to the police and going out to dinner, we went to Mega Maxi. I took the opportunity to buy Ben's present – a Spanish scrabble set. Fortunately we remembered to buy presents for Caz and Jesse – Ben had assumed I would buy these and I had assumed that he would. Whilst waiting for the clock to strike midnight, we conclude that it's been a mad day and one not to be repeated except of course the Christmas dinner that was rather splendid and not a Brussels sprout in sight – Ben and I share a mutual dislike for these. At midnight I give him his present. From the shape he guesses what it is and tells me before opening it. Giving in to the temptation to beat him up, I point out the fact that at least I did wrap his present. Mine was not even wrapped but it was sweet of him to replace my large coffee mug that broke on the trip last week. I suggest that from now on we only play scrabble in Spanish – he is not amused and heads off to bed. We bid each other goodnight as we have another early start.

Sunday 25th December…

On this cloudy morning Ben and I are bouncing up the hill behind the school with Clare and Woody and Woody's parents who have come over for a holiday. Clare comments positively on our increased fitness levels – I too am impressed. It is the perfect way to start Christmas day. Clare is talking about their plans to leave Ecuador next summer and work elsewhere in the world. She has been here for almost eight years and I sense that she will really miss the place. As we walk I share my disappointment at having to cancel the Cotopaxi climb – during last week's training we learnt that climbers were doubling back as the snow was waist high and impassable. There are no signs of the weather improving. Clare suggests postponing it until after the New Year and holding onto her climbing gear – we are a similar size and Clare has loaned me all her stuff. I tell Clare about Stuart's attack as I respect her perspective. After listening to the details she raises her eyebrows and sighs. From her reaction, I know that she too wonders if the incident could have been avoided and if Stuart will mature through this experience – how can a group of people in their thirties be at such differing levels of maturity and understanding. After the short walk Ben and I grab quick showers and head off to join the other teachers for lunch.

***

I knew that I would revisit the area of forgiveness and I guess Christmas day is as good a day as any. Stuart has again been sharing his thoughts and feelings about what happened to him. He is in a state of real anger and wants revenge. He tells me that he wants to harm those who had harmed him – he is asking himself if he is capable of violence and tells himself that he is. He tells me that he has spoken to a friend at home who has tried to encourage him to see the situation from the perspective of those who robbed him, to understand their position and to forgive. He is not ready to do any of these things as he believes that even if he had nothing he would not turn to violent crime, so why should anyone else have a right to do so. I want to point out the contradictions. I want to ask if he has ever experienced having nothing or being exploited. I want to point out that we can only speak from a privileged position and that we can never really know what it is like to live as the poorest in one of the poorest countries. I want to suggest that the act of forgiveness would benefit his health and restore his well being – and that by not forgiving he is continuing to let the crime control his emotional, psychological and physical well being. But I say nothing. Over time I'm sure he will reach his own conclusions, whatever they may be. I think about Faith who really opened my eyes to forgiveness. On this cold day I know that she will be warm as I did send her the blanket that I promised. I smile knowing that she will be reunited with her family by next Christmas. Perhaps Stuart should meet Faith.

Ben has intuitively dragged me away from the situation and offered me a drink – as usual he is driving, so I accept – I want to put aside the world's troubles for the remainder of the day. The lunch is superb – turkey is served with the usual trimmings and a really flavoursome homemade stuffing – and it is a pleasure to overindulge a little. The rest of the afternoon is spent playing board games, drinking too much and just chilling out. The teachers tell me about the forthcoming trip to Baños to celebrate the New Year. Although night clubs and eardrum bursting music is not my scene (and never has been), as we have postponed climbing Cotopaxi, I accept the offer to join them. As is customary, Ben is in several minds including his need to catch up with school work, consider going to the rugby function etc – I know that he would rather go on the trip but I don't want to influence his decision. It is late evening and Ben and I head home. Ben thanks me for being his social secretary – since when I ask myself – and sorting the Christmas lunches. I respond by simply saying, 'Home James.'

Tuesday 27th December...

It is the crack of dawn and I find myself wide-awake on this cold and damp day. Yet again it has been raining overnight and I can still hear it drumming against the metal bars on my window. It has been four days since the three of us returned from our mountain trip and the rain has been relentless with the exception of Christmas morning. It has been wet, wetter or wetter still. The house has felt so cold and damp that both of us have been walking around in sleeping bags – how pathetic would we be if it was really cold! Even Ben had a hot drink which is unheard of.

I pull back a curtain and examine the horrid weather – going off to the warmth of Baños tomorrow is suddenly very appealing. Looking at the heavy grey clouds I think about Cotopaxi – today is the day that we had originally booked to do the climb and by now would have been heading for the top. Ben has re-scheduled the climb for the end of January and we plan to do some more training in the first few weeks of the New Year. It is likely that two guys will join us on this challenge. Clare and Woody have kindly offered to do some ice climbing practice on the Cotopaxi glacier. This will be good as I have not used crampons or an ice-axe since my trekking trip to Greenland.

***

Lying in my warm bed, I randomly access my memories and find myself thinking about the nuns, the children and the volunteers at the project. I smile to myself as I picture the nuns in their light brown loose fitting habits that hide their rotund bodies and the wimples that cover the wide brimmed sun hats. I wonder why these women became nuns and chose to work with children. During my time at the project, they never hugged the children, never comforted them and never laughed or played with them – I had had visions of them playing football with the children and just chilling out. But there again my only real experience of nuns, up until working at the project, was that of a large nun who knocked me down during a football tournament – speed and skill didn't work so she used brute force instead. Now I ask myself if they are capable of offering more than food, shelter, clothing and strict discipline. Is it their faith that requires this or is it simply the effect of dealing with a helpless situation year on year – would any of us become like that in a similar situation. Still I have no answer.

I wonder what has become of my children, are they still there, have they returned home, are they well, and are they happy? I miss them all – it was a privilege to have spent time with them and I know that I will never forget them. On my last day, I went in bearing gifts for all the children that I had worked with. I felt like Santa Claus with the huge sack that I dragged into the project. Over the previous week I had taken over the living room floor as I prepared each gift – every night Ben stepped over the parcels as he made his way around the room. I carefully spent every dollar of the funds donated by the school and by friends back at home. The gifts were well received – Antonia just kept looking at her gift bag in disbelief – I suspected that she rarely received presents – and the smile just said it all. Jacson kept opening and closing his mouth and reminded me of my fish. The white metal aeroplane meant the world to him and he repeatedly said, 'It's mine, it's mine, it's mine' – as he showed it to everyone and anyone.

Jairo showed his two new little cars to everyone, pulled out his own two from his pocket and lined them up on the dining table. José gave me a big hug and said that I can't leave – he admired his new pens and writing pad. Anna Gabriella accepted her bag and momentarily her magical smile returned. In her bag I included a jewellery making kit but I really wanted to get her the Harry Potter collection. Even the pressure cooker had run out of steam and smiled when he received his gift. In the gifts for the boys I included marbles and for the girls I included hair bands – I remembered how much delight it brought to their faces when Iki included them in the little bag of sweets. For the benefit of the younger children, I bought 10 new story books and gave them to the teacher. She gratefully accepted the books and told me that I should not leave the project – over the weeks I found that she did care about the children and had started to follow our method of teaching. For all the children I bought sweets and chocolate lollipops – the ones with the howling whistles. By the time I left all the children were walking around whistling. I'm afraid the little devil within made her appearance. Scary Nun was not amused but I was grinning like a Cheshire cat – over the weeks I had continued to keep the lead in scrabble (at present it is 8-6 to me) and had had a lot of practice with the old grin.

My fellow volunteers have restored my faith in the human race. Even the two new young volunteers that joined as I was leaving were committed to the children and wanted to make a difference, no matter how small. It was a privilege to have met and worked with Iki and Michael and I know that both will continue to make a valuable contribution to society.

***

I leave my inner world and get a coffee before sitting down at the dining table to do my Spanish homework – I seem to have taken up permanent occupancy of this space. This work is in preparation for a two hour lesson that I have booked for this morning with my new tutor, at my new school. I am continuing with the Spanish lessons until I leave but decided to switch schools when I discovered that my previous school was owned by Europeans – I want to support the local businesses. During my introductory visit to the school, I was given a load of worksheets that I agreed to complete before my first lesson – it is more advanced grammar and quite challenging. Ben still thinks I am a girlie swot and still refuses to converse in Spanish – although he has asked me to get him a copy of the course book that I am using. I suspect that I will be back from my lesson before he makes an appearance. I will drag him out of bed for some lunch before our friends arrive.

***

It is mid afternoon and four of us are sitting around thinking of topics and questions for the next pub quiz. At the December quiz we agreed to write the one for February. Sadly, we dropped down to fourth place by two points. We were surprised to learn that American Pie was dedicated to Buddy Holly and Chameleons change colour to match their moods not their surroundings – how will I get over the trauma of being misled by my biology teacher! It was a good night out and Ben decided that winning one drink was not enough and won three consecutive shooters during the quick fire round on Shakespeare – he didn't even do A level English literature. Unknown to Ben, I have put him forward as the quiz master – I will let him know just as I go through the departure gates. I want categories on art and cartoons or things to do with childhood, Ben is more logically focussed – like how many countries would you pass through if you went east to west along the equator, Tamara is keen on scientists and inventions and Stuart is more concerned with playing pool on the six inch pool table that Ben got as a present at the staff Christmas lunch. After a few hours and several cups of Yorkshire tea – my stocks were replenished by a huge parcel that came through the post from home – we are nearly there and decide to watch Finding Nemo in Spanish. Ben is still engrossed in the quiz – he will be ensuring that all the questions are worded without any ambiguity and will no doubt go off on many internet diversions whilst doing so – and three of us leave him to it and turn on the DVD.

Friday 31st December...

It is the remains of the year that is shortly to be left behind. The sun is setting once again for the final time and a new dawn is appearing for the first time on the horizon as the world populations look ahead to new dreams, hopes and aspirations. I have taken this opportunity of solitude away from the group of people who have afforded me their hospitality and friendship over the past few weeks to reflect and be still. I am sitting alone on the only sun lounger on the roof terrace of the hostal Posado del Arte. I am surrounded by rich green mountains. As I take in the remains of the final sunset of the year, I allow my body, soul and spirit to absorb its warmth. At the same time, I let my body feel the gentle cooling breeze blowing across the terrace. As I look out at the cascading water, bouncing merrily down the rock face of the luscious mountains, and listen to its soothing rhythmic sounds I close my eyes and find myself thrown back in time.

I am lying face down on a hidden secluded beach cove in Abel Tasmin and feeling the trickle of grains running through my toes as I repeatedly dig my feet into the sand. The midday sun is warming my torso and legs and the cool sea breeze is blowing gently across my semi-clad body. I lift my head and focus ahead on the distant horizon, where the sea and sky join in union and become one. All is still and quiet and there is no sound other than that of the waves gently greeting the driftwood lying across the sand before me.

To this place of stillness, I come with new questions, new thoughts and new reflections. For some there will be no sunset, no new dawn, as for them the sun has already set for the final time. They will not see this final sunset of the year, or feel the warmth of the sun or the coolness of the gentle breeze. Those broken of spirit, heart and soul will not see the sunset with absolute clarity against a clear blue sky. Theirs will be a hazy experience, not knowing if the sun has set and concluded the previous year and not knowing when the new dawn will finally appear. I ask myself what becomes of these souls, how are they healed, how are they made whole again, to once again enjoy the sunrises and sunsets of their lives. And what of those who are oblivious to the passing of time, unaware that this precious resource is passing like sand through an hour glass, never to be reclaimed.

Alas, I find no immediate answers and my thoughts are interrupted as members of the group return from their respective day trips and join me on the terrace. One member notices my notepad and asks, 'Is it a journal?'

I am not sure what to call it. Is it a journal, is it an epic novel or is it just the ramblings of a journey that started with nothing more than a drawing pin. I say nothing for I know not what to say.

Over coffee I comment that this is the final sunset of the year. Someone replies that there will be others. I say nothing further but think about all those for whom there will be no others. Idle chatter interrupts the setting sun but through it all I watch the perfect circle vanish behind the ridge of the mountains. As the last person leaves I am alone again and enjoy the magnificent light that the sun has cast across the surrounding mountains. I continue to be cooled by the gentle breeze rustling through the leaves of the surrounding trees whilst watching the cascading water and listening to the distant birds. My heart concludes that nature is a beautiful thing as I make my way down to my bedroom to prepare for the evening's activities.

***

Following an hour long Salsa dancing lesson at the nightclub, we have all returned to the hotel to ready ourselves for an evening of celebration. My super cool dress sense will comprise a cream top, dark green canvas trousers, a terracotta scarf and a cheap wooden necklace that I purchased earlier in the day – I enjoyed watching the woman make the gifts in her little market stall and parted with two dollars without bartering. My attire will be complemented by my worn-out blue, white and grey running shoes – the very shoes that carried me over the finish line of the 25th Great North Run in a finishing position of 4321. It's either my trainers or my Scarpa walking boots as I have no other shoes with me – I had come to Baños with the intention of climbing the active volcanic mountain and doing other sporting activities and had forgotten about the clubbing and dancing. And not just any old dancing but proper Salsa dancing.

Saturday 1st January...

It is the first day of the New Year and I am sitting on the swing chair on the veranda of a bedroom that I am sharing with a British schoolteacher. Sadly, she was unable to join in last night's celebrations due to a high fever – I suspect that she picked up a bug whilst we were white water rafting in dirty brown water. Following a poor quality expensive meal, we walked around the town to absorb the sights and the sounds, before heading to the nightclub that we had frequented for the past two nights.

Now, as I look back, I decide that it was indeed a sight to behold but too much to absorb and retain. The town was packed and all around was the sound of music and celebration. Children and adults were walking around in colourful masks and street vendors were selling their wares – garlic enriched cooked meats, bright pink candyfloss, popcorn, masks and fireworks amongst other things. Men were dressed in women's clothing and I wonder how many closeted gays used the opportunity to express their sexual identity in this safe environment. Some people were dressed in animal outfits and were groping people as they walked past. Many were imbibing cheap wine, although no one seemed completely drunk and out of control. On every street there were effigies of varying sizes and made from various materials that were to be burnt at midnight, to say goodbye to the previous year. I am intrigued to know more about the significance of such actions – symbolically what are people really doing. Are people seeing the year out, burning away negative experiences or burying the past? Are the sizes of the effigies significant? If so, there were some enormous issues that needed to be dealt with. I ask myself if it is so easy to dissolve the past in this way and conclude that if it works for some people then who am I to question its merits. Yet in the midst of this fiesta, there were those who sat alone on the pavements and watched as the Mela unfolded before their eyes. They were in it but yet not able to be a part of it. The poor and the disabled were begging from the rich, perhaps hoping for greater generosity at this time of year, but they received none and some were turned away harshly. I looked out for the old blind drummer and his frail wife that I had observed for the past few days but they had left for the day.

In the nightclub, we watched the locals entertain with some impressive dancing – definitely strictly come dancing – to some exceptionally loud music. Despite my hour's training and being told that Indian people have a genetic predisposition to rhythmic movement I refrained from partaking and declined several offers – some experiences are best left to others to experience and excel in. I decided not to drink, as I wanted to absorb the atmosphere. At midnight there was no Old Lang Sine – although the Brits did do a rendition later on. Instead, as far as the eye could see, whole streets were ablaze with fires, upon which effigies were being flung in great numbers and lighter fuel perfumed the atmosphere. Fireworks were going off in all directions. Fireworks that are normally set vertically in soil and lit several feet away from people were being lit in the hand and pointed towards the sky – many went off in all sorts of unintended directions. Just in case people hadn't had enough of a fire display, some firelighters came along and put on a road show, juggling great balls of fire and spilling turps everywhere. We all moved to the balcony for safety as well as a better view of the street below. Unperturbed by the fires and choking black smoke everyone was greeting each other with the saying, 'Feliz Año Nuevo.'

Sitting on the balcony and declining the offer of cheap champagne, I could not help but wonder if this would be a pyromaniac's dream scenario. Cars were driving up and down the streets and casually passing through the sky high flames. At one stage the fumes and smoke were so overpowering that most people headed indoors – and I reached for my inhaler. At the end of this mad hour, light coloured clothing was no longer light coloured, everyone reeked of smoke fumes, but the dancing and partying resumed. I laugh as this type of fiesta would not even be contemplated back in the UK, let alone planned and executed. Apart from one minor fracas the evening at the club passed without trouble.

Saturday 7th January

It's gone 4pm and I am sitting in the cold refuge that serves both Iliniza Norte and Illiniza Sur. The four of us that will be tackling Cotopaxi in a couple of weeks time decided to come and do an extra weekend's training – three others from the school decided to join us, including Paula.

The planned 7am start resulted eventually in an 8am start from the car park at the base of the two mountains – this perturbed me as the weather generally tends to be worse in the afternoons and I wanted to leave enough time so that we would be descending the mountain peak before 1pm. It took 3 hours to reach the refuge rather than two due to the extended rest stops. At the refuge three people were clearly starting to feel the effects of altitude and were in no fit state to go on but three others wanted to continue. I agreed with Ben that I would walk with the other three and he would remain with the two at the refuge. We set off just after 11.30am. After only a further 50 metres of ascent, one of the group members declared that her headaches had become worse and that she felt dizzy. As I could see Ben I advised that she go down the scree slope towards him. That left three – seeing someone go down the scree slope alone disturbed me as did the thought of a split group. I was even more perturbed when Paula said that she could not remember the word for gloves at the refuge and now was struggling to remember everyone's name – but she wanted to go on. I said that we should go back down but Stuart offered to accompany her to the top adding that she would be okay. What a dilemma I was facing – adults make their own decisions but I could not help but think that Paula was not in the best of states to make the right decision and that Stuart was being reckless. I decided to return to the refuge perhaps in some vain hope that my actions would help them to come to their senses and that they would follow me down – Ben spotted me and met me part way up. I explained the situation and we agreed that I would wait at the refuge and he would take everyone else down to safety.

That was over 4 hours ago. The weather since has deteriorated, darkness is descending and there is no sign of them. I ask myself if I should have been more assertive and insisted that everyone went down and that the group remain as one group – but what can you do when everyone is an adult and responsible for their own decisions no matter how irresponsible the decisions might appear to you. Given Paula's state, perhaps I should have been more insistent with Stuart and got him to realise the potential severity of the situation. Now I can do nothing but wait – the refuge has filled up with climbers and their guides over the last few hours. All are intending to climb Illiniza Sur tomorrow and all know that I am worried. The host at the refuge wonders off and makes a call – having reassured me earlier he too is now worried. No doubt a search party will be sent out if necessary and no doubt I will be left waiting in this now very cold room without the means to remain warm overnight. I feel helpless as I have no means of contacting Ben who will no doubt be sitting, waiting and worrying – sensibly I suspect that he has sent the other three off in the second jeep. One of the climbers offers me a hot drink which I gladly accept – his face mirrors my worry.

I am suddenly distracted by the yells for help coming from outside and my heart sinks to the depths of an impending loss as I see Paula walk in without Stuart. My face must have said it all as she quickly said, 'Stuart is fine, he is helping to carry down a lad who broke his ankle whilst climbing. We and another couple stopped to help him and his friend.'

I am unable to respond as all I can think is that it could have been one of them given Paula's disorientation and her insistence to continue. After a silent walk in the dark we are back at the car park – Ben is relieved to see me and gives me a big hug which I gladly accept. He knows and I know that we can't discuss the matter until we are alone. The experience reinforced my belief that the mountains are to be respected.

Saturday 21st January...

It's 5.30am and six of us are sat eating a candle lit breakfast of stale white bread, strawberry jam and warm instant coffee at the El Porvenir hostal in the Cotopaxi National Park. This is the last weekend of training before the big climb, but right now, I would quite happily forego food for a mug of fresh coffee and an extra hour in a warm bed. In contrast, Woody is fully recharged and probably has enough energy to run up to the glacier. As we finish breakfast and walk out into the chilly air towards the jeeps, the first rays of dawn light appear. The day gradually wakes up as we drive up to the car park and see some of the best views of Cotopaxi – the almost perfect conical snow-capped peak is set against a cloudless blue sky – and make several photos stops. It is certainly the perfect day on which to be doing the climb and we can just make out the dots of people attempting their ascent.

After a morning of playing – playing is the right word because that is exactly what we have been doing albeit with crampons, ice-axes and ropes – we are taking a well earned rest. Sitting on the glacier and playing with my axe, I find myself recounting an experience involving an ice-axe. I tell the group that a colleague had kindly offered to lend me a pair of crampons and an ice-axe for my trip to Greenland. I accepted the offer and agreed to collect the items from his office on Chancery Lane – this was on one hot summer afternoon. Kit in hand I descended the escalators to join the other peak time suits. It was the usual 5pm tight squeeze – with the usual aromas of armpits disguised by the usual expensive perfumes. However, within a few minutes I found myself with more than usual personal space – enough room in fact to swing an axe! The penny was dropping in very slow motion – my axe was generating the personal space. The crampons came in their protective bag but the ice-axe didn't. Slow motion gave way to pure panic and my mind was playing out a number of scenarios. Do I say, 'It's OK folks, I'm not mad, it's just an ice-axe.' Do I hide the axe under my jacket – no, no, no, this would make the situation appear far worse. Do I make some cheap and facetious remark like, 'I got the axe today,' – in reality this wish had not yet come true. Or do I act normal – what would be normal in such a situation – obviously carrying an axe on the underground is an every day occurrence! I tried to make myself as inconspicuous as possible by standing nonchalantly in the corner and holding my axe like a walking stick. As I listened to the shuffling feet and uncomfortable coughs and watched the side way glances, I knew that I had triggered people's fears and misperceptions. I was glad to be getting off a couple of stops later. This experience happened before the events of 7/7 – the day that marked the end of innocent stupidity and perhaps gave birth to the schizophrenic society where big brother watches your every move and is still non the wiser. The group find the story highly amusing and Ben comments, 'It could only happen to you.'

As the cold wind is gathering and the weather is closing in, we call it a day and head back to the car park. On the way down Ben and I decide to try out the new Indian restaurant that I have found in Mariscal – it's called Speedy Gonzalez and is run by an Indian who speaks Punjabi.

Sunday 29th January…

I'm now at 5,520 metres – information courtesy of my guide who insists on dragging me up this awesome uninviting mountain. I estimate that this is probably 18,500 feet and 500 feet above the cover provided by my insurance policy. The route is A1 with no traversing and tough enough to test the thighs of an elephant. We are blessed with atrocious weather – rain, snow, sleet and not to be left out the wind has joined in – and my clothing is caked in ice. However, I feel very warm under all my layers. For the past 300 metres – ever since Ben turned back due to exhaustion and I got roped to Stuart – my brain has been very preoccupied. Many would argue that the only thing the brain is capable of at this altitude and in this glorious weather is putting one foot before the other. Not mine I'm afraid. This journey started many months ago with Ben. We trained for this climb together. There were times when Ben's legs were jellified and I watched out for him, there were times when I couldn't breath and Ben watched out for me and there were times when we were both knackered but each encouraged the other. Yesterday morning Ben carried most of the gear from the car park to the hut knowing that I was unwell – this was very evident as I was the last one to the hut. He prepared all the meals and allowed me to sleep as much as possible so that I could be ready for the climb. We were roped together and set off before the other two. When he couldn't go any further he encouraged me to get to the top and handed me the pigs before turning back with the other guy. Pigs is a game that you play with two plastic pigs and was often dragged out in the evenings on the training weekends. We thought it would be good to take the pigs and play a game at the top – but now we won't be doing this.

This suddenly feels like a solitary journey, a solitary climb – besides Ben had agreed to drag my body down the mountain should I die and scatter my ashes across the ocean – there is no one to do this now. I stop in my tracks – the guide is now very annoyed and reiterates that I am acclimatised and fit enough to reach the top. I tell him it's my asthma – it is restricting me but not enough to prevent me from continuing – but I know that he is not convinced. Stuart tells me to get to the next ridge before deciding to quit – looking at him I ask myself if he would ever take useful lessons from his life experiences, the mugging and the reckless adventure on the mountain seems to have had no impact on him. I actually feel like saying, 'This climb ended when Ben turned back and I can't do it without him,' but decide to keep silent. After a few more paces, I tell the guide that I'm turning back. Stuart is not amused; he sulks all the way down and several times hits the snow in anger. I return to the refuge and find Ben fast asleep on the bunk bed next to mine. I wake him up by throwing bits of ice at him. He sticks his head out of the sleeping bag and bursts out laughing when he sees that I am covered with ice. He hands me a warm woollen hat and asks how it went. 'The asthma let me down,' which isn't the truth.

I crawl into my sleeping bag. We chat for a while about life, the world and the universe before grabbing some sleep. We talk about the places of stillness and solitude in our inner worlds and our friendship suddenly feels cemented.

Wednesday 1st February...

The alarm of my Casio mountaineering watch is bleeping me awake. It's 4.45am. It's imperative to not only stay awake but to physically haul myself from the comfort of my bed or otherwise risk missing my plane. Shivering, I crawl out of bed and head towards the kitchen. My stomach rebukes the thought of food at such an early hour but accepts a cup of stronger than usual coffee to satisfy the cravings of the brain. The caffeine is failing to kick my brain into action. As I reach the dregs at the bottom of the mug, Ben staggers out of his bedroom. He decided last night that he would get up at 5am and do some school work – actually, knowing my love of mornings, it is his way of just making sure that I am up. Still half asleep, he says good morning and asks if I have my antibiotics – he insisted that I got some after the Cotopaxi climb as I had had a persistent cough for over a week. I show him the packet and shove it back into my fleece. He looks at the pile of work on his desk and concludes that another hour in bed is far more appealing than writing a whole load of reports. As he heads back towards his room he offers to be woken up again should my taxi to the airport fail to materialize. I simultaneously bid him good morning and goodnight.

Just before leaving, I place a $10 note and some sweets on the dining table for Gladys. As I drag my well worn black canvass bag down the very grassy drive – it has reached a height of ten inches – I tell myself that I will never commit myself to such an early start again. It's now 5.15am on this chilly morning and everything is so still – is it a time when the human race is still and perhaps at peace with itself. Even the tom cats are quiet. I've had two sleepless nights this week thanks to the tom cats that have sat under my window and screamed at the female cat next door. I got up twice in the middle of the night to douse them with water. In the end I just threw the water over the bitch next door and that put an end to the howling as she promptly went indoors. I felt a pang of guilt as the neighbour works in Ben's school. The guilt however dissipated as I enjoyed the silence and fell asleep for a few hours. I refrained from disclosing my actions to Ben.

I watch the dawn of the first day of the new month as I wait patiently for my ride to the airport. Standing outside the gate, I realise that time is passing like grains of sand that cannot be gripped in the hand and I can't believe that a twelfth of the year has already gone. However, the time has been well spent. Looking around, I notice things that I hadn't noticed before. The double front gates have a little 8 by 4inch hinged door through which it is possible to identify your visitors – I have used this gate for four months and never noticed this gadget. I see that nature is attempting to reclaim this territory – weeds and grass have fought their way through every crack and crevice. Up the street, I see that the guard is missing from his little telephone booth sized box. I watch as two women run past the top of Pontevedra. I reprimand myself for failing to retain my running fitness whilst in the country. My one and only run at Papallacta was sufficient to deter any further attempts.

I notice the, 'Darshan Singh Villa,' sign – I never did pop in and say hello. And now I never will. I,m suddenly struck by sadness as I know this holiday to the Galapagos marks the start of the end of my stay in Ecuador. When I return I will be saying a final goodbye to the people that I have met over the last few months. Ben has organised an overnight trip with the teachers to Papallacta. I've arranged various lunches with fellow students and volunteers. Ben and I will have a meal with Ximena, Paul and their baby daughter Cise, who arrived in early January – I've enjoyed my afternoon teas with Ximena whilst she has been on maternity leave. Ben and I have agreed to end as we started, with a meal at the local Italian and a game of scrabble – the score is level at 8 games all.

It's 5.45 and I'm opening the front gate with the intention of waking Ben. Just then a car turns left into Pontevedra and pulls up opposite the gate – it's my lift.

Wednesday 1st February

The 4.45 AM start is seeking revenge and I could quite happily drop my head on the shoulders of the blond guy sitting to my right and nod off. I could even do the same to the elderly gentleman to my left but the shock might finish him off. But no, I must exercise restraint as I sit amongst seven complete strangers, seven foreigners, in this badly air conditioned Baltra airport lounge and pay failing attention to the tour guide. He utters the words, 'Good journey?'

I remember getting on a plane at Quito airport, I remember the look of horror on a fellow passenger's face when I asked him to turn off his mobile – the plane was taxiing to take off and he had ignored all the requests made by the cabin crew, I even remember being applauded for my actions and hiding my embarrassment behind a travel guide. But beyond that it seemed like an endless journey.

'Hola, what is your name?'

'Que, what?' is my reply as I realise that the guide is talking to me.

I learn that Blondie is from Belgium and called Pierre. The old guy reintroduces himself as Jo from Canada and NOT America. The group also includes three Swiss women and a couple from England and that is the extent of the information I have absorbed. But I have already concluded that there are likely be three groups within this group of seven.

Relieved of $100 each for the park entrance fee we are taken by bus to the port to wait for our dinghy ride to the boat. As we disembark we are welcomed by two sea lions that are casually sunbathing and a jet black Iguana that is strolling aimlessly back and forth across the concrete platform. The tour guide, who is called Rafael, tells us that we will need to wait here for a while due to some bureaucratic complication. Totally overcome by the tropical heat and the lack of sleep, I go and sit quietly on one of the two wooden benches – the other is taken up by one of the sea lions. I am only a few feet from both. As I wait, from behind my shades, I take in the behaviour of tourists as they arrive. It is a sight to behold and is certainly beyond belief. Collectively each bus of tourists that arrives is making more noise than my street children ever did and my ears are hurting from the high pitch screams of excitement. I watch as group after group of adult tourists with fantastically expensive cameras take hundreds of photographs of the two sea lions. I'm sure size zero catwalk models would be red with rage. Curious to see if I have missed something, I lift my shades and look at the two sea lions. But no, they are just sea lions doing what sea lions do – not a fat lot. Rafael takes an uninvited glimpse into my inner world and smiles – I return the smile and then cover my eyes once more. The sea lions are totally unperturbed by this strange behaviour. 'Estoy con tigo,' – I'm with you, I mutter under my breath, as the sea lion lying on the concrete opens hers eyes and looks up at me.

The best comment is made by an ample American pensioner in grey pigtails and knee high shorts who upon disembarking screams, 'Gee, are these put here for us.'

In turn I stare at the two sea lions. The one on the park bench must weigh at least 400kg and the one at my feet about 150kg. The sea lion on the concrete opens one eye and looks up at me again. 'I'm not with them,' I find myself saying apologetically to the sea lion.

But suddenly I realise that I am. My status has changed from that of temporary resident and volunteer working with street kids to that of tourist – psychologically I had not prepared myself for this transition. I pull my cheap El Nacional baseball cap further over my eyes and turn my gaze towards the distant horizon.

***

After seeing many coaches of tourists come and go, we eventually leave the two sea lions and take the dingy to our boat the, 'Sea Cloud,' just in time for lunch. Lunch is certainly tasty but huge. I can't resist thinking that after a week of three meals a day, each comprising two to three courses, some tourists will have a lot more in common with the sea lions. I might stop looking like my scrawny street kids.

After lunch we are allocated cabins and briefed by Rafael about the week's activities. We start by heading off to the first Island – Isla Plaza Sur.

After a short dingy ride we disembark at a concrete landing platform. I feel overwhelmed as my five senses compete with each other. My eyes are taking in the hundreds of sea lions engaged in different activities, the iguanas and the birds, as my nose deals with the scent of the mammals and my ears the bellowing of the male sea lion that is making it clear that it is his territory and that he is boss. This noise is amusing as it sounds as if the sea lion is drowning every time he comes up for air. I can taste the sea salt on my lips and feel the warm damp breeze that is being soaked up by my clothes. I have never been greeted by a colony of sea lions before but perhaps greeted is the wrong word as quite frankly all the creatures ignore our presence and continue about their business. Only the baby sea lions seem faintly interested, as they bounce towards me and watch with amusement as I stagger backwards to keep the official metre distance from the wild life, whilst avoiding stepping on the iguanas that blend beautifully with the surrounding environment. As we stroll around the island on demarcated paths, we are exposed to wild life that I have only ever dreamed of seeing. On one section of the Isla we are allowed to wander around and enjoy the sights. I use this opportunity to sit in the middle of an imaginary isosceles triangle near the edge of the cliff. The apexes of my triangle mark the resting points of three male sea lions attempting to sleep in varying postures. One that is badly scared following a shark attack is resting on its side. Another is resting peacefully on his stomach and the, 'Cliff hanger,' is resting on his back and looking extremely suicidal. For ten minutes I watch a yellow breasted wobbler attempting to re-enact the story of David and Goliath. It is randomly pecking away at each of the sea lions. Several times they flip him away just to find that he is back pecking away at a different body part. Twice he has flown into a sea lion but simply bounced off. My enjoyment is interrupted as the group is led back to the dingy and back to the boat across the choppy sea.

Thursday 2nd February...

After a 7am breakfast, ours is the first dingy heading towards the second Isla called Española. As we approach the shoreline, all I see is a stretch of sea lions sunbathing on white coral sand – lumps of drying grey matter. Rafael informs us that we are free to meander on this beach – in other words we are no threat to the endemic life. I decide to trudge off to the other side and find a quiet spot amongst the sea lions. After a cursory glance in my direction they close their eyes and resume their positions in the sun.

I sit and watch the baby sea lions doing what the young of all species should do, that is, play without a care in the world. Some play with their mothers whilst seeking refreshments. Some mothers although initially expressing annoyance at being disturbed by their young soon roll over and allow them to feed. The young adults are allowing themselves to be rolled into the shoreline on the crests of the incoming waves and then swimming out again so that the waves can bring them in again – I want to join in with the fun but I quash my enthusiasm as I picture myself being crushed under a wave of sea lions. These sea lions seem content, at peace with themselves and their world. They co-exist alongside all the other species.

My time of stillness and peace is shattered by the engine noise of two dinghies that are approaching the shoreline – the sea lions too are perturbed by the polluting sound. I strip down to my swim wear, grab my snorkelling gear, and dive into the water in search of sea life. I allow myself to be consumed by the silence of the sea and the sea life within as I trace the movement of marine iguanas around the rocks near the cove. My own mouth mimics that of the fish as I watch the great show. I am reminded of my pond life and laugh as I imagine myself popping my head in the water to say hello to the goldfish and native newts.

***

After lunch we head off to another section of the Isla in search of a different endemic variety of iguana and other wild life. I am struck by the wonderful autumnal skin colours – the reds, greens and terracotta blend beautifully. Rafael points out all the places where the iguanas have laid their eggs – this would not be obvious to the outsider. Walking around, I am mesmerised by the comical blue footed boobies that are performing the mating ritual before our very eyes. Suddenly I understand the male tourists sporting their, 'I love my boobies,' tee shirts – so it had nothing to do with their man boobs. I am saddened as the last of the albatrosses is struggling to take off – Rafael tells us that it will not succeed in fulfilling its migration journey. I watch sea lions riding the high waves and crash landing on the land on the rocks. Momentarily, I'm frozen solid as I watch a sea lion fly onto a rock in front of me and lift his upper body against the distant horizon – is it really possible to be so intimate with these creatures. I capture his silhouette in the perfect evening light and thank him as I walk on.

***

Sitting here on the lower deck I am thinking about Jo who has just headed off to his cabin to change for dinner. Whilst writing I observed Jo drift off to some music to another place, a place of great sadness. As the piece of music came to an end he returned, eyes glazed with tears. I wonder where he went and what triggered the sadness. I wonder if the heart surgery that he underwent only a year ago has focused his attention on his own mortality. I wonder if he is still coming to terms with his recent retirement. Confucius says, 'Old age, believe me, is a good and pleasant thing. It is true that you are gently shouldered off the stage, but then you are given such a comfortable front stall as spectator.'

At 68 Jo is freed of his duty to both society and family he can travel the world as a spectator. I turn my attention to Pierre, the youngest member of the group – yesterday we celebrated his 23rd birthday – who has left the security of his home in Belgium to experience life in South America. In his late teens he survived a near fatal illness and I suspect this experience has and will influence his future life. Listening to his story I know that he is still making sense of why he survived his illness – he is angry that he survived yet so many people do not. I could not and did not offer any explanation – he will find his own answers and purpose in life.

Saturday 4th February...

It is a disturbing shock to the system to be woken by shouting at the crack of dawn in the middle of the ocean. This is precisely what is happening this morning as I dignify my body with a pair of joggers and top. It's only 6am. As I reach the deck I am relieved to hear the words, 'Dolphins, dolphins,' rather than, 'Abandon ship, abandon ship.'

As I rub and focus my eyes on the distant horizon I am bewildered by the sight before me for it is indeed a sight. Hundreds of dolphins are doing a merry dance to the rise of a new dawn. As we come within 30 metres it seems as if they are accompanying the ship. It is the most wonderful natural acrobatic show I have ever seen. As the dolphins pass behind us I conclude that it is one of the best dawn's I have ever witnessed. I know it is going to be a memorable day.

After breakfast we go off to Punta Moreno on Isla Isabella and walk across the solid lava – what an experience. Rafael tells us that Volcan Sierra Negra had been active only last October but now it is hibernating again – it is so harmless, so tranquil. After this short trip we take a dinghy ride around the Isla to see the wildlife up close and personal. Penguins, marine iguanas, herons, flightless cormorants, sea turtles and sea lions are sitting within a few feet of our dinghy – posing beautifully for our cameras. My favourite is watching the birds eating the limpets off the backs of iguanas – one gets cleaned and one gets fed in the process.

After lunch we have another opportunity to be one with nature in the silent world of the sea. I am happy as both Jo and Pierre – who had been reticent about snorkelling – join in. Sea lions swim close by, penguins shoot past before I could acknowledge their presence and giant turtles passed quietly under my flippers. Sadly the snorkelling is cut a little short as the sea becomes turbulent and obscures the viewing. So we head back for an afternoon snack and English tea – three meals a day is clearly insufficient food.

The close of this day is indeed as wonderful as the start – the sighting of whales is followed by a perfect sunset. The sun is going down over the distant horizon in a blaze of glory, lightning up the sky high above with glorious reds, oranges, blues and purples and reflecting its beauty in the sea below. There is complete silence and stillness with the exception of a gentle warm breeze. As I go down to my cabin to carefully store this memory, Pierre comments, 'There are no words.'

I say nothing as indeed there is nothing to say.

Sunday 5th February…

The setting sun has just crept away but left behind a cushion of crimson cloud that is hugging us beautifully – minute by minute over the last 30 minutes the sky has become more and more beautiful. Pierre and I are sitting silently on the deck and dangling our feet over the edge of the boat. The group's willingness to be kicked out of the cabins at the crack of dawn was rewarded by an uninterrupted viewing of giant tortoises and Iguanas, hawks and Darwin birds on Isla Isabela – a ship carrying 100 passengers arrived as we all escaped to Isla Fernadina. In the afternoon, keeping one step ahead of the crowds, we all headed for the best snorkelling spots to enjoy the sights of the underworld – sights that can only be inadequately described in words. Groups of sting rays, perfectly synchronised, simply glided through the water before my very eyes. Seals came a bit too close to my body – maybe my black swimming costume and black flippers intrigued them. Near some rocks I spotted more small penguins diving into the water and vanishing at great speeds. The day was crowned by a family of killer whales that accompanied the ship at a safe distant – what a trip, what an adventure.

Tuesday 7th February…

After an hour's snorkelling where we saw big fish with big teeth in the aqua coloured sea, three of us have been granted permission to explore the young lava on this particular island without the company of the guide – the rest of the group were not too enamoured and have chosen to go for an extended snorkelling session. The sun is blazing down from a cloudless pale blue sky and in this heat Jo and Pierre are applying factor 50 to their very white sun sensitive skins – I stick to my usual factor 35. As we stroll across the lava, Jo and I tease Pierre as he is unable to distinguish the word working from the word walking and has invented his own word that is almost an amalgamation of the two. Yesterday Jo spent hours helping him to pronounce the two words with limited success. As we walked up and down a sandy beach in the warm rain, Jo chanted, 'Wa, wa, walk, walking,' followed by the words, 'Wo, wo, work, working' and then asked Pierre to repeat the chant. Oblivious to the rain, they continued in this manner for almost thirty minutes – it was like watching a live comedy sketch and I just fell about laughing.

The lava has stirred the child in each of us and we stop every few minutes to take photographs of shapes and patterns that the flow has created – we imagine seeing seals, iguanas, birds and even the head and shoulders of people. It is definitely the place to create a million imaginary stories. I suddenly have a brain wave and ask Pierre to lean forward onto the lava and as he does so I photograph his shadow – he too has his imprint in the lava. Jo joins in – so I capture him as well. Pierre has offered me the use of his camera as the batteries in mine refused to go on and on and on – my charger is accumulating dust back in my room in Quito. After 45 minutes a distant shout is calling us back to the dinghy – reluctantly we head back.

Wednesday 8th February...

The sun is rising in the early morning sky and we are in the dinghy taking one last trip before leaving the Galapagos. But do you really leave this place I ask myself as I watch the pale reds of the dawn sky...

Friday 10th February...

It is just before midday on the last day of my trip. Having finished my last Spanish lesson and said goodbye to my tutor – I have promised to e-mail her a recipe for an Indian curry, I have stopped at the Coffee House Company café for the last time on this particular trip. I am sitting at my usual table under the only tree on the forecourt. As usual I am taking in the local life whilst sipping a freshly squeezed juice – the guard acknowledges my presence with the usual smile. I know that I will miss this city, the city that has been my home for several months. I will miss all that which has become familiar – the traffic noise, the pollution, the culture, the people and the way of life. I will even miss the cracked pavements and potholes. As I take notes of my surroundings, my cheap pen provides me with a new challenge – the ink has travelled from the tip to the lid – and dies a slow fading death as I write – I wonder if this is the effect of altitude. Last night I was with the teachers at Papallacta. It was the perfect place to say goodbye to everyone. Paula and I enjoyed the champagne and chatted about life, the world and the universe – as one does under the influence of alcohol. Clare talked about her forthcoming wedding in England – Woody proposed at Christmas – and Woody's new job in Europe that will start in the autumn.. Some endings are never easy and the fun time was tainted with sadness – I will miss this ex-pat community.

I pull out another pen from my bag. It too has suffered the same fate. I throw the pen back into my bag and decide to just commit everything to memory. I look around and watch the tourists – it is always easy to identify the ones that have recently arrived by their nervous dispositions and collection of literature – information on Spanish schools, accommodation and safety.

Michael strolls across the road – his hair definitely needs cutting. As he joins me at my table he is eager to update me on the happenings at the project. I get him to choose something to drink before continuing. The good news is that Anna Gabriella, Jairo and his sister Maria did return home by Christmas. Anita was moved to a specialist unit. Jacson was sadly dispatched to another home – as soon as he reached the age of 10 the nuns got rid of him for being difficult. The rest of the children are still there. Michael is pleased to tell me that he has left the project and will be volunteering in a project working with disabled children before doing some travelling. I have enjoyed working with Michael and I hope that over the forthcoming years we keep in touch. We say goodbye after we finish our drinks – I am due to meet Ximena this afternoon before going out for dinner with Ben this evening.

Saturday 11th February...

It is 7am and Ben is sitting at the computer and I am packing the last of my belongings – I have left some clothes for Gladys' grandchildren. My flight bag is full of Spanish literature and probably weighs about 15kg – I came only with a dictionary but am leaving with an encyclopaedia worth of material. I have packed the Christmas presents that Ben bought for his nephews in Otavalo. The two of us took off on a day trip to Otavalo during the fiesta de Quito. Instead of walking around the nearby lake we decided to become tourists for the day and enjoy the offerings of the now almost tourist market – in one day we bought all our Christmas presents. In my bag I find space for my large coffee mug. Ben laughs. I simply say, 'It would be rude to leave my Christmas present.'

We are sitting at a café at the airport and Ben asks if I have my passport and ticket – after the event as always. I pull out both and wave them at him. The scrabble is lying on the table unopened – the score will remain 8 all. We conclude that the meal at the restaurant was as good as the first and just the place to say farewell.

It is nearly time to leave. As Ben waves me through the gates I smile and think, 'A relative stranger at the Arrivals gate but very much a dear friend at the Departures gate.'

It has been a wonderful journey and I could not have asked for a better travelling companion. I will miss him.

Tuesday 17th April...

On this glorious spring day the gentle breeze is creating a shower of pink and white confetti and all the gold fish are scoffing flakes in the morning sun. I'm sitting in my usual spot with a Christmas mug of fresh coffee and contemplating when and how to break the news to the pond life – we are all going on a new journey.

Lightning Source UK Ltd.
Milton Keynes UK

178179UK00002B/195/P

9 780955 988608